# Vignettes of Taiwan
Short Stories, Essays & Random Meditations About Taiwan

by Joshua Samuel Brown

Vignettes of Taiwan
by Joshua Samuel Brown

Copyright ©2006 ThingsAsian Press
All rights reserved under international copyright conventions. No part of the contents of this book may be reproduced or utilized in any form or by any means, electronic or mechanical, including photocopying and recording, or by any information storage and retrieval system, without the written consent of the publisher.

ThingsAsian Press
3230 Scott Street
San Francisco, California 94123 USA
www.thingsasianpress.com

ISBN 10: 0-9715940-8-2
ISBN 13: 978-0-9715940-8-1

# Table of Contents

- 1 Foreword
- 7 The Curse of Interesting Times: Taiwanese History Made Simple
- 15 Shotgun Wedding
- 21 Please Leave Now
- 23 Buddha Box
- 25 Stinky Tofu
- 27 The Night Market Has No Class
- 31 Please Be Reverent
- 33 Expatriate Preserve
- 35 Taking Five Finger Mountain
- 39 Seven Counting Me
- 45 Money Comes to Hakka Town
- 49 Eventually It Will Rain
- 51 Shake, Rattle and Roll
- 57 The Unhappy Affair at Happy Kids Kindergarten
- 61 Mister Happy Gets His
- 65 Skinny Asses
- 69 Bless the Beasts and Pass the Betel Nut
- 75 Humble Mahjong Loser
- 81 Betel Nut Ingénue
- 89 The Fruit Lady of Shita
- 93 The Master has Fast Hands
- 95 Your Friend, Khalil
- 101 Lantern Festival
- 103 Death by Cholesterol
- 107 Drought
- 111 Strange Foreign Person
- 115 Fight Club
- 123 Love Hotel Etiquette
- 127 Water Running Up
- 129 Green Island: Ready for the Big Time
- 135 Nighthawks at the Night Market
- 139 On the Mooch in Dihua Jie
- 143 Last Dance for the KMT
- 147 Taiwan Speaks Up, Damn the Torpedoes
- 153 Isle Formosa - An Inaccurate Historical Account

Special thanks to all the folks in Taiwan who helped make this book possible (only some of whom actually had stories written about them): Kyle, Zippo, Long Long, Tammy and Philip at Pristine, Don at Topics, Hsiao Mei, Catwalk, Phelim, Mike (currently exiled in Shanghai), the Mooney family, and of course, the Yeh family for giving me a place to call home.

Note on the romanization of Taiwanese place names:

In Taiwan, the romanization of Chinese names is complicated and heavily steeped in politics. Prior to the late 1990s, Taiwan used the Wade-Giles system, allowing names of places to be read by people unfamiliar with Chinese characters. The Wade-Giles system was also likely politically acceptable, being different from the Hanyu Pinyin used in China. In recent years, the Taiwanese government has attempted to switch to a third system, called Tongyong. However, not all cities and counties in Taiwan agree with this change, resulting in a confusing set of circumstances in which the romanized spellings of certain place names may be spelled differently on signs and maps around the island, depending on the political leanings of the sign painters or map makers at the time. Rather than pull my hair out over the issue, I have attempted to consistently use the most well known romanization of place names as of September, 2005. Whether these will still be correct next year, let alone five or ten years in the future, is anybody's guess.

For more details on the romanization of Chinese characters, check out www.pinyin.info

# Foreword

I stepped out of the passenger terminal at Chiang Kai-shek International Airport in Taoyuan and was slapped by what felt like an enormous palm of hot, wet air. It hit me with a body blow then caressed me with muggy temper, wrapping itself around my body like a damp terrycloth robe taken from the dryer too soon. It was August, 1994, and I was fresh off the plane on my first trip to Asia. I had 1,300 dollars in traveler's checks, a heavy suitcase filled with clothing ill suited for the climate, an English-Mandarin dictionary and a head full of visions of living out my own personal David Carradine / Kung Fu Asia fantasies for a few years on the island of Formosa.

I was twenty-four years old and thousands of miles away from home, with a heart still smarting from the wounds of an unrequited love affair. I'd made a vague commitment to myself that I'd stay for two years, then bum around Asia, then go to Japan to make my name as a big-time international something-or-other. I was in a strange and humid land, with a very heavy suitcase, the number of some friend-of-a-friend I barely knew, insufficient funds and zero prospects. I was at that moment the happiest man alive.

My decision to come to Taiwan was, like much else in my life up to that point, based largely on random occurrence and cosmic coincidence. I'd graduated from a small university in upstate New York with a Bachelor's degree in English two years earlier. For years the American media (and perhaps its collective unconscious as well) had been yammering petulantly about how the Japanese, with their strong work ethic and air-tight economy, were poised to buy half of America out from under our feet. As strong and confident as the Japanese had become, however, the country seemed to have a manic craze for all things American, and were paying top dollar for white faces with smooth tongues. The yen was booming, and many were the tales of hapless and otherwise unskilled recent college grads like me who'd struck gold in the land of the rising sun.

But Japan was not my destiny, and dumplings played a role in turning the path from beneath my feet.

I'd been eating dumplings at Golden Pond Dim Sum for years. The small café on Clinton Street in Rochester was one of those rare Chinese restaurants you sometimes find outside of major metropolitan areas that actually serves Chinese food (as opposed to the American version of Chinese food that nobody in China would even recognize). I was thumbing through a book called *Teaching English in Japan*. The book had a large picture of Mt. Fuji on the cover, and Ms. Ma (the woman who ran the place with her sister) was giving me the hairy eyeball. I was a regular customer, and the sisters had always treated me well, but the vibe today was all wrong. Coming over to refill my teacup, Ms. Ma muttered something distinctly unpleasant in her own tongue, a hiss that sounded like "*errr…ban…gui*!"

She looked away from the book and leaned on the table.

"Why you thinking about going there? If you want to teach English, you should go to Taiwan."

I knew next to nothing about Taiwan, and what I'd heard led me to see it as a kind of vast factory churning out medium quality consumer products and bargain bin tech gizmos while millions of aging, disgruntled soldiers milled about waiting for the call from a long-dead general to retake the mainland from the communists. I made some sort of non-committed noise, and drank some tea.

"Taiwan is my home," she continued. "Very beautiful. Much more beautiful than Japan."

"Is the airfare expensive?" I asked tentatively.

"Eh…" she answered. "I fly back maybe every other year. I call my agent for you. Maybe can get you a good deal."

A few days later, following more dumplings and conversation with the sisters Ma, I was sold. Truth be told, it wasn't the sisters' tales of idyllic childhoods in Taiwan that convinced me.

Nor was it their descriptions of heartbreakingly beautiful mountain scenery, vast repositories of cultural relics waiting to be discovered, or encouragement about how well I would be treated by Taiwanese people - "We love Americans." The facts that steered my decision were of a more pragmatic nature; counting every penny I'd managed to save over the past year in perpetually-depressed upstate New York, I had just over two grand. Assuming half of that would be needed to get me across the big drink, I was cutting it close in either place. Cheaper than Japan by a wide margin, Taiwan it would be.

A decade later and here I sit, a seasoned international something-or-other, writing an introduction to a book of stories about a place that feels more like home to me than the city in which I was born. Except for a couple of overnight visa trips to Okinawa, I never really did make it to Japan (where despite a ten-year economic downturn, a cup of coffee is still more expensive than in Taiwan). This book of stories, essays, meanderings and images is dedicated to the place that took me in all those years ago, treated me as well - if not better - than Ms. Ma had promised, and never quite let me go.

Joshua Samuel Brown
September 8, 2005

# The Curse of Interesting Times: Taiwanese History Made Simple

Taiwan, Republic of China?
Taiwan, Province of China?
...or will simply Taiwan do?

Taiwan's oddly ambiguous status is one of the anomalies of the geopolitical world map. The mentioning to someone with a basic CNN knowledge of geopolitics that I've lived there a bunch of years often leads to some variation of the following question:

"So what's the deal with Taiwan? Is it an independent country or part of China?"

Except to die-hards in either opposing camp (those firmly pro-Taiwan independence and those advocating reunification), the question of Taiwan's status defies any kind of pat answer. The best way to make sense of Taiwan's somewhat ambiguous status is to understand its history.

Taiwan was originally called *Tapanga* by the ethnic Malayo-

Polynesian aboriginal groups who inhabited the place before Chinese settlers arrived in the sixth century. At first, the Chinese government was less than keen on the idea of its citizens settling the island, going as far as to outlaw the practice. Thus, the earliest Chinese pioneers tended to be people with little to lose on the mainland, such as desperate peasants from the southern coastal provinces or pirates looking for a place to nest between raids.

In the 1600s, European imperialism to the Pacific began in earnest, and Taiwan entered her first period of colonial occupation at the hands of the Dutch and the Spanish. The Ming emperors, after nearly a millennium of meditating on the issue, finally changed the prohibition policy and encouraged emigration to Taiwan. The aborigines during this period were either "assimilated" into the dominant Han culture, or pushed eastward into the mountains, as the population of Chinese immigrants rose to nearly 3 million.

In the seventeenth century the Ming dynasty fell to the Qing dynasty, and one Ming loyalist chose to make a last stand on Taiwan. Koxinga, as he was known, retreated to the island with the remnants of the once powerful Ming navy. Though Koxinga was able to drive the Dutch off the island, his men could not long withstand the might of the Qing fleet. After being assimilated into the Qing dynasty, Taiwan continued on as a Chinese backwater for the next two centuries. In 1895, with the Qing on its last legs, Taiwan was ceded as war booty to Japan by the Empress Dowager Cixi. The Taiwanese, not wishing to be handed over to a foreign power, declared a Taiwanese Republic. The Japanese had other ideas, and after landing a fleet in northern Taiwan, drove southwards, crushing the fledgling government and integrating Taiwan into its burgeoning empire.

During the Second World War, Taiwan was used as a major staging ground for the Japanese, and many Taiwanese were drafted into the Imperial forces. With the defeat of Japan, Taiwan again found itself in the position of war booty, this time handed over to Chiang Kai-shek's Nationalist government. While many Taiwanese initially celebrated their liberation from Japan, the bonhomie between native Taiwanese and their latest liberator was short lived. In 1947, a confrontation between an elderly cigarette vendor and a Nationalist soldier led to a massacre of Taiwanese by Nationalist soldiers. This confrontation is now remembered as 'the February 28 Incident' or simply '2/28.'

Following 2/28, Taiwan entered the dark days now remembered as 'the White Terror.' Thousands of Taiwanese students, labor activists, intellectuals and others became targets of systematic imprisonment and repression by the ruling Nationalists. In one of history's many ironic twists, this period of tyranny saw Taiwan blossom from a third world agrarian economy into one of Asia's leading exporting nations. While growing by leaps and bounds economically, politically Taiwan was frozen in time. But outside, the world was changing. Across the strait, China's tumultuous post-revolutionary fervor was on the verge of exhausting itself, and America, Taiwan's staunchest ally, was beginning to look past the island's (then) population of 19 million and consider the possibilities presented by the mainland's billion-plus. For the Kuomintang (KMT) government of an entity called "the Republic of China" (ROC), the era when they could sensibly lay claim to being the rightful government of all of China was fast coming to a close.

The seventies brought a decade of great change for the fortunes of the ROC. In 1971, the Republic of China lost its UN seat to the People's Republic of China (PRC). In 1972, lifelong red-baiter Richard Nixon made his landmark visit to China, where he stood on the Great Wall and uttered the now-famous words, "It truly is...a great wall." While hardly a master of poetic platitudes, Nixon, through his trip, would forever change U.S.-China relations, and in doing so, inexorably alter Taiwan's world standing. By the decade's close, Chiang Kai-shek was dead, the U.S. had switched its recognition from the ROC to the PRC, and the era of strategic ambiguity in Taiwan's relationships with China and the rest of the world had begun.

Taiwan began the eighties in a state of political shock. Externally, the ROC had just lost its place in the international community, and, it seemed, the most powerful ally in the world. Internally, as their standards of living rose to reach that of other first world Asian nations, the Taiwanese were clamoring for political freedom to match their economic status. For the ruling KMT, it seemed that being anti-communist China would no longer be sufficient. For Taiwan to regain some semblance of legitimacy on the world stage, it would have to become Democratic China in fact as well as theory. In 1987, Taiwan's state of martial law was lifted. For the first time in nearly two generations, Taiwanese people were free, if they so chose, to refer to themselves as Taiwanese rather than Chinese.

Shortly after issuing the edict lifting martial law, Chiang Ching-kuo, son of Chiang Kai-shek, died. He was succeeded by Lee Tung-hui, Taiwan's first native-born president. Each succeeding election would see the once-outlawed Democratic Progressive Party (DPP), advocates of formal Taiwan independence, gain seats in both the Legislative Yuan and the National Assembly. In 1996, Lee Tung-hui was re-elected in Taiwan's first freely held direct presidential election, despite (indeed, some contend, aided by) Chinese 'military exercises' held dangerously close to Taiwanese waters. During Lee's final term in office, he would make a number of proclamations seen by the PRC as proof that the outwardly stalwart KMT *apparatchik* was actually firmly in the pro-Taiwanese independence camp.

In 2000, Taiwan elected former Taipei mayor and pro-independence candidate Chen Shui-bian of the DPP, ending more than five decades of rule by the KMT. As the dust from this hotly contested three-way race settled, there was wide consensus that outgoing President Lee had sown the seeds of discord within his own party to make Chen's victory possible. In parliamentary elections held in December 2001, the DPP won enough seats to make the KMT a minority party in the country it once ruled with an iron fist.

Sovereign nation, renegade province or something in between - a detailed account of the history of a place as culturally rich and politically intriguing as Taiwan in 1500 words is impossible. This then is a summary, intended only to answer the question so often posed by people who've never been to Taiwan but are dubious of the rote cut-and-paste tagline, so often found at the end of any story about Taiwan, in which its history is summarized with a variation of the sentence, "Taiwan split from China in 1949."

There's an old Chinese blessing, cliché almost at this point, but appropriate - "May you live in interesting times!" In bringing this summary to the present day, it's worth noting that in 2004, Chen Shui-bian was re-elected by a razor-thin margin in a hotly contested election. In 2005, KMT leader Lien Chan made a trip to China for the first meeting between Nationalist and Chinese Communist Party leaders since 1949.

While Taiwan meets the qualifications for statehood as defined by the 1933 Montevideo Convention (which defines a state as any territory possessing a permanent population, a defined territory, a government and a capacity to enter into relations with the other states), all but a shrinking handful of countries around the globe dare recognize Taiwan as a nation for fear of earning the wrath of an increasingly powerful People's Republic of China. And for the Chinese, the question of reunification is not a matter of if, or even necessarily how - only when. What the future holds for Taiwan is unclear save for one certainty - it will be interesting.

Lest anyone forget, the blessing cited above is also considered to be a curse. ❖

# Shotgun Wedding

Something in Mr. Cheng's demeanor makes me very uncomfortable, sitting as he is in a throne-like chair carved from a single piece of wood and scrutinizing me the way an army sergeant might a new recruit. He pushes a plate towards me and utters several words in thickly-accented Mandarin. The only word I catch is *chi* - eat, so I stuff another moon cake into my mouth, my third in ten minutes. His daughter Shi-wei - or Suzie as she'd been introduced to me hours before by my friend, Nevets, at the reception desk of his English school - sits next to me smiling happily. I flash back to my first meeting with Shi-wei that afternoon. When my new best friend in Taiwan had introduced me to his young receptionist, she immediately invited me to take a spin with her around the town of Tsaotun, get some dinner, and then come back to her house.

"It's a traditional Chinese home," she'd said, and I pictured rolling tiled eaves, stone pillars inscribed with Chinese characters, perhaps a pair of jade lions standing watch by the ornately carved wooden doors.

"Be careful," Nevets had warned me as we left, and I figured he was talking about motorcycle safety. Surely he couldn't have meant be careful as in don't knock up my receptionist. I'd only been in Taiwan a month, but I already knew enough to realize that Shi-wei was a traditional girl. After we rode around town and had dinner at an open air roadside café, I offered to ride with her to see this "traditional Chinese home." It turned out to be a low slung wooden structure, certainly Chinese enough (the roof was indeed curvaceously tiled), but not quite the Qing palace I'd expected. The presence of her waiting father made me realize that light petting was not to be on the evening's menu, though things were about to get heavy in a different way.

Satisfied that I've had enough moon cake, Mr. Cheng begins what I can only assume is a lecture, spoken in a rich, authoritative (and to me, a non-speaker of Mandarin, completely indecipherable) voice, pointing to certain visual aids hanging conveniently on the wall behind his wooden throne. Shi-wei provides ongoing translation.

"Father wants to make sure you know who this man is," she says, pointing to a framed portrait of Generalissimo Chiang Kai-shek. Though a newcomer to the world of 20th century Chinese politics, I know who Chiang is, or was. The Generalissimo, though dead for decades, had once led the Kuomintang, one side of the Chinese civil war that lasted through a good chunk of the 20th century. His leadership left much to be desired, and owing to a combination of avarice and tactical incompetence, it had led to the KMT being banished to Taiwan less than five years after the surrender of Japan, despite heavy monetary and military support from America.

But the delicate gold embellishment set lovingly around Chiang's photograph tells me that Mr. Cheng might not share my views on the Generalissimo's shortcomings. "Chiang Kai-shek," I say, using his English name, adding in blocky, incorrect Mandarin, "*yi-hau-ren*," (a good man). Mr. Cheng nods, smiles and continues.

"This is President Sun Yat-sen! His vision was betrayed by communist bandits, who stole the mainland from the good people of China!" translates Shi-wei as her father gestures reverently to the portrait of the young revolutionary doctor who helped to overthrow the corrupt Qing dynasty. I smile and nod with what I assume to be a safe reverence.

"And this," says the father, sweeping his hand before the map, "is our country, China. The Republic of China." He pronounces the last words carefully, so there can be no mistake that he means The Republic of China, and not any other similarly named entity. "Do you understand?"

Shi-wei beams her smiling face in my direction as her father scrutinizes my own for some sign of comprehension. Again, I smile and nod. Shi-wei smiles and nods. Mister Cheng does not smile, but merely looks satisfied. He leans over and speaks quietly to his daughter, who nods enthusiastically.

"My father says that he likes Americans, and is very open-minded. But it is important for you to understand our history if you are to join our family."

"Erk?" I say, a chunk of moon cake suddenly lodged in my esophagus.

"Mr. Nevets says that you have just come to Taiwan, and are not married. Is this correct?"

I cough, sputter, and wash the moon cake down with a hastily swallowed thimble full of scalding tea.

"I have to go now," I announce, standing up with great rapidity. "I have to work early in the morning…in Taichung City…very, very far away."

I smile inanely. Mr. Cheng looks perplexed. I grab my nylon jacket from the coat hook and make for the front door of the traditional Chinese home followed closely by Shi-wei. Her face is frozen in a waxen smile as I kick start my Sanyang 125 motorcycle.

"Tell your father I say thanks for the tea and moon cakes," I yell behind me before dropping the clutch and skidding away at extremely unwise RPMs. The last thing I hear is Shi-wei yelling something at my back.

"Call me, OK? I really think my father approves!" ❖

# Please Leave Now

If you're a last minute grocery shopper in Taipei City, you may notice in certain supermarkets a song playing over the public address system. The song plays in a loop, from about 30 minutes before closing until whenever the last customer leaves. It is harmonious in every way, a lullaby almost, save for one thing; with every loop, the song gets louder. At 10:30, it's at a pleasant enough volume. By a quarter-to, the decibels are getting noticeably less comfortable. It's as if someone is trying to tell you something. Dally too long trying to decide between the silken and firm tofu at 10:58 and you may feel as if you're being yelled at. In 28 minutes the message has gone from a subtle one to a piercing scream. But the lyrics, whispered or shouted, have not changed. It's a prerecording of a melodiously sung and heartfelt thanks from the management to the patrons. The lyrics of the song contain a gentle reminder that management and staff have been on their feet all day, and builds up to a rising, thundering crescendo with the song's final operatic refrain:

"*Wan aaaaaaaaaaan! Wan aaaaaaaaaan!* (*Bai tuo-huo-huo!*) *Ming! Tian! Jian!*"

"Goodnight! Goodnight! (We beg you!) See you tomorrow!"

This is the Taiwanese shopkeepers' way of telling you politely to please leave now. ❖

# Buddha Box

I acquired the blessed thing on an express train from Hsinchu to Taichung. A middle aged man with shaven head, orange robes, serene smile and half closed eyes, pulled it from an orange satchel and pressed it into my hands. I thanked him and smiled for a moment before realizing, newly arrived and still perplexed by the ways of the East, that some contribution was in order. Pulling a fifty *kuai* note from my pocket, I smoothed it reverently before placing it into his bowl. He smiled, bowed his head and continued down the aisle.

Jet black and made of plastic, the box was clearly made to fit the average palm of an average hand. It looked like an old style transistor radio, one with strange markings all along the front and an image of a charcoal brazier printed in gold ink alongside its single round speaker. On the top edge of the box was a grooved volume knob, which I switched on. Melodic feminine voices sprung forth.

*Naaaa - ma aaa - mi to-o-o fo, nama ami to fo, nama.*
*Naaaa - ma aaa - mi to-o-o fo, nama ami to fo, nama.*

A woman sitting in the seat across the aisle smiled at me, and though I'd felt at peace before switching the box on, I now felt especially tranquil. I held the box in my average sized palm as the melodic chant continued its loop eternal (or at least until the battery gave out). I felt one with Taiwan, at one with the universe. My only concern was how they'd gotten a choir of nuns into the box in the first place, and what might happen should they suddenly decide it was time to leave. ❖

# Stinky Tofu

*Cho dofu*, or "stinky tofu," is the Taiwanese snack that separates the men from the boys, the women from the girls, and occasionally, the women from the men. *Cho dofu* is tofu that's been fermented to a nice degree of pungency, then deep-fried and served with pickled cabbage and hot sauce. *Cho dofu* is very much a Taiwanese delicacy. Carts selling it can be found at any night market, and in most neighborhoods and towns. Generally speaking, you can find the nearest *cho dofu* stall with your eyes closed, as the stuff is quite rank. Though tofu is usually thought of as a healthy alternative to meat, those making regular pilgrimages to the local *cho dofu* stand in the name of health are kidding themselves, since the stuff is as deep fried as deep fried gets, usually in animal fat, but some stalls catering to vegetarians use vegetable oil. Though I resisted it for the longest time, I finally gave in and had some with one of my students. (Taiwanese people enjoy bringing foreigners out for *cho dofu*, seeing it as a bonding ritual.) Eventually, I developed a taste for the stuff because it was cheap and filling. Though I knew it wasn't exactly healthy, I justified eating it regularly by telling myself that it was served with pickles, and thus counted as both a vegetable and a protein. Describing the smell is difficult. To those who don't like it, *cho dofu* is a cross between limburger cheese and fried sweat socks; to those who do, it's a whiff of pure heaven. ❖

# The Night Market Has No Class

Once upon a time Formosa was a poor place, and the majority of the island's inhabitants were farmers, merchants and craftspeople. In those days, a meal out for those lucky enough to afford such an extravagance, was often taken *al fresco*, and consisted of a bowl of rice with some vegetables, and maybe some pork or seafood. But nowadays, Taiwan's humble roots are a thing of the distant past, and in the capital of Taipei, restaurants catering to all social and economic classes can be found in great abundance. But at the night market, meals are still eaten in the open air, and all class distinctions are transcended in the national pursuit of gastronomic pleasure.

Taipei is filled with night markets, some bigger than others, but even the smallest of these boasts food carts in the dozens. There's scant room for parking in the blocks surrounding a night market, so cars, along with class distinctions, are left outside. On any given evening at the Shita Night Market, named for the nearby Shita University, the casual observer is likely to find harried mid-level salary men bumping elbows with taxi drivers at the metal counter of a stand serving stinky tofu, a national delicacy the flavor of which is both distinctly Taiwanese and definitely an acquired taste.

Further down the street you might see students slurping down bowls of *bing sha* (sweetened shaved ice with fruit) alongside secretaries from nearby office blocks letting their hair down after hours.

Across the river in Shilin, home of Taipei's oldest and most well known night market, it isn't surprising to come across a group of well-dressed CEO types sitting alongside denim clad scooter mechanics at a greasy counter eating greasy oyster pancakes smothered in sweet sauce. To the outsider it may seem odd, this convergence of dissimilar strata of society, but to a Taiwanese there's nothing at all strange about seeing the elite rubbing shoulders with the *hoi-polloi*. The night market does not discriminate; it is the closest thing to an egalitarian meeting ground to be found on this island of 21 million, an oasis of authenticity in an increasingly materialistic, face-based society. ❖

# *Please Be Reverent*

Losers can write history also, as an afternoon stroll through the innards of the Chiang Kai-shek Memorial Hall Museum confirms. The memorial itself is perhaps Taipei's best known landmark, a bulb-topped blue and white monument to the man who lost the world's most populous nation despite the patronage of its most powerful. Occupying the entire ground floor, the museum celebrates the life and times of the man whose greatest achievement was liberating China from his own rule. In addition to the obvious displays one would expect in a museum honoring the life of a political leader - life sized portraits of the Generalissimo engaged in the sorts of things men of his stature did, such as surveying battlefields from horseback, meeting with kings and statesmen of the era, or simply gazing benevolently - the museum also offers glimpses of other facets of the man's life, like ornately crafted swords, ceremonial uniforms, and custom made bulletproof automobiles.

Students of modern Asian history will find the interpretation of the events of the Generalissimo's time, as offered by the museum, most interesting. Praised highly is the bravery of the Kuomintang troops who with Chiang at their helm drove the Japanese from China's shores. Nary a word is mentioned of the communist soldiers who, commonly accepted history tells us, played a major role in that struggle. And the fact that the detonation of two atom bombs over Japan proper might have played some role in the decision of Japanese high command to withdraw from China is likewise not mentioned. A visit to Chiang Kai-shek Hall is proof that you don't need to win the war to write your own version of history - you just need to escape it with enough money to build a museum.

In the upper section beneath the blue dome sits a gigantic stone statue of the Generalissimo, poised in eternal respite but ever ready to rise up and retake the mainland should the opportunity present itself. Please be reverent, as the sign suggests. Do not attempt to disturb the guards by following them as they march in synch, or by making silly faces at them as they stand perfectly immobile at their guard posts. Unlike those at Buckingham Palace, these guards keep their guns loaded. ✤

# Expatriate Preserve

The neighborhood south of Shita University is where young, fresh faced students from abroad come to study Chinese, immerse themselves in local culture, and prepare themselves for a life of hair-tearing frustration in the world of East-meets-West business. It is here that we find in great abundance members of the expatriate species, engaged in the various rites and rituals peculiar to them and their ilk. An afternoon spent in the Shita Expatriate Preserve is indeed an elucidating experience to those who wish to understand the species. Taiwanese are advised to follow certain common sense precautions to help ensure that their trip to the preserve is both a pleasurable and educational experience.

If one follows you, do not panic. The attention span of average expatriates is notoriously short, and they will most likely lose interest when more attractive members of any bipedal species catch their notice.

An expatriate may approach you offering a "language exchange." Do not, under any circumstances, accept the offer; decline politely, but firmly. Such arrangements are never without strings.

Should an expatriate follow you outside of the confines of the preserve, duck into one of the many conveniently located McDonald's, buy a cheeseburger, and leave it unwrapped on a nearby curb. This will usually distract the expatriate long enough for you to make your escape.

Of course, under no circumstances should you take them home with you, no matter how cute they may seem at the time. Many are the tales of naïve locals who have taken expatriates home, only to be reduced to flushing them down the toilet once they realize just how much trouble they are.

While these are most likely urban myths, it may account for some of the strange sounds one often hears emanating from deep within the sewers of Taipei.

# Taking Five Finger Mountain

Since coming to Taiwan one year ago, I have aged at least three years. Aside from the tropical and not so tropical maladies I have contracted, the sheer weight of time has come crashing down upon me like cartoon pianos that had been dangling twenty stories from a flimsy rope. My legs, once solid muscle from my years as a New York bike messenger, are now almost normal-looking. The prideful things of adolescence are memories now, but I spend little effort in self pity about aging. Indeed, today I've decided to regain some lost pride; today I will take the carbon fiber mountain bike that I bought three months ago (and left to gather dust in the garage) for a ride into the mountains.

Mountains are tricky, however, because they tend to appear close while actually being far. To get into the mountains I have to ride out of the city first, up Guangfu Road for about 16 kilometers before coming to the town of Chudong, or East Bamboo. Said to be one of the oldest towns in northern Taiwan, Chudong has many buildings built during the years of Japanese occupation; crumbling and blue, they are beautiful but disliked because of the colonial time they represent. I stop at the base of the nearly impenetrable mountains that I am about to penetrate and have an iced papaya milkshake before beginning my climb up the nigh-impossible road. It begins easily enough, a gentle incline past Buddhist temples and collapsing red brick houses. The road becomes steeper, weaving up and around mountains, running next to a wild blue river fed from a thousand springs. The road rises farther to a fiendish incline, and even the few scooters that pass by seem to be doing so with difficulty. The road forks, one tine heading into valleys and the other heading higher up still. An arrow pointing towards the high road shows the characters *Wu zhi shan* - Five Finger Mountain.

Something inside of me needs to take this road, its fresh air mingling with just a hint of the burnt brake pads of a thousand descending cars. The road snakes steadily upward, seven hard kilometers of mountain, dotted with shrines and pagodas to one side, and a sheer drop on the other. Passing drivers shout words of encouragement - "*Jia you. Jia you.*" Somewhere close to the top, two barefoot kindergarteners run alongside me, as if challenging me to race. I beat them to the next curve before passing out.

I regain consciousness lying under a small red gazebo looking out over the mountains. A small black dog is licking the sweat from my face. I am not at the peak, but the peak is in view, maybe a kilometer further up an even steeper stretch of road. I toy with the idea of making a final push, as a younger me would have felt obliged to do. But then I take stock of the situ-

*Taking Five Finger Mountain*

ation. I'm lying on my back on a tea bench, heart pounding, lacking the strength to even stop this strange dog from licking my face. Here, I decide, is good enough. As I think this, I have a realization. The key lies not in surpassing, but in accepting one's own limits.

Hours later, I arrive home after a fast ride down followed by a fatigued slog through Hsinchu traffic. Well after sundown, I take a shower before smearing tiger balm all over my body. As I fall into an exhausted stupor, one thought comes to me - my bar mitzvah oath was taken prematurely. Only today am I truly a man. ❖

(This story was written in 1995. I never again attempted to take Five Finger Mountain.)

# Seven Counting Me

There were five people living in the Yeh family's house, six counting me.

I'd come to Shuangxi by accident. Though I'd originally intended to live in the city, the one-temple Hakka village on the outskirts of Hsinchu felt right to me, and I could tell the place would provide a more authentic space in which to spend my first couple of years in Taiwan. The wife of my friend, Andrew, was a local, and had learned through the Hakka grapevine that the Yeh family had a tatami apartment for rent. The thought of renting to a foreigner hadn't occurred to Mother Yeh. On our first meeting, she scrutinized me with a critical eye, expressing a litany of objections, which Andrew dutifully translated.

"She's worried that you won't keep the place clean."

Through Andrew, I told Mother Yeh that I was fastidiously tidy - an exaggeration, but I wasn't a slob.

"She wants you to know that this is a family home. You can't bring strange girls here."

I told Andrew to tell her that I was a nice Jewish boy, hoping that she hadn't read *Portnoy's Complaint*. This was a good call on my part. Though I didn't know it then, Hakkas, as one of China's most historically persecuted clans, feel a certain empathy towards Jews. When she learned of my Semitic origins, Mother Yeh became more open to the idea of letting me move in.

"She asked me if I thought you'd have any problem living on a building's fourth floor," Andrew said, "but I went ahead and reminded her that Westerners don't consider four unlucky."

In Chinese, the number four is highly inauspicious, as its pronunciation (si) is nearly identical with the word *si* - death. Many Taiwanese wouldn't consider tempting the fates by living on the fourth floor. But the number four meant nothing to me. I smiled and held up four fingers and said, "*Mei wenti* - no problem." Mother Yeh smiled back and held up four fingers of her own. I was puzzled until Andrew provided translation.

"The rent is 4000 NT a month." I accepted, not caring whether the rate was auspicious or not.

So now there were six people living in the Yeh house, including me. I saw little of the father, Yeh Hsiao-lu, those first few months; he was working with the capitalist tenacity for which Hakkas are famous, pre-selling units in an apartment block that had yet to be built on a patch of land on which, until recently, grew only papayas. I saw the grandparents more often; grandfather spent much of the day sitting in front of the television drinking tea and watching the Taiwanese stock market channel. He had a lot of money invested, but was never too absorbed to yell *Jiashi, lai he cha*! - "Joshua, come drink tea" - if he heard me coming down the stairs. Grandmother was usually outside in warmer weather, helping her daughter Reijui (who I called Auntie Yeh) sell betel nut from the booth out front. And Chien-chiu, the youngest son (the only one still living at home, the other two having gone off to college) would come up to my room and play Chinese Chess every now and again. The Yeh parents had high hopes that my presence would somehow help Chien-chiu to learn English, as if having me around might trigger in the lad some kind of osmosis learning reflex. But the heart of the chubby eleven year old wasn't really into English; he found it more fun to help me practice Chinese

"Say it again! Say you're going to Taipei with your girlfriend!"

"*Wo qu taibei gan wo de nu peng you.*"

I'd repeat, and he'd giggle like a lunatic. It was only much later that I realized that I'd been pronouncing the word "*gen*" - Chinese for "with" - as "*gan,*" which means "fuck."

Other than these encounters, and the occasional meal with the Yeh family, I was pretty much left alone. The interior of the house was larger than it appeared from the outside. The front half of the ground floor was taken up by an interior garage with polished stone floors. Inside of this space were parked various motorcycles and Yeh Hsiao-lu's shiny white BMW, which he'd purchased in the early flushes of newfound real estate wealth. Behind this was an enclosed kitchen and living room, the social hub of the house. It was here that guests were entertained, meals eaten, and copious quantities of Wulong tea and sunflower seeds were consumed. The grandparents had their own apartment in the back that I had never seen, but assumed was roughly the same as my own place upstairs. The third floor had an extra bedroom that the oldest sons would occasionally use when they came home from school and a large hall with tile floors and a pool table that nobody ever used. The parents lived on the second floor with their youngest son. And I lived on the fourth, in a self-contained tatami apartment that took up the back third of the floor. It was a good place to live. I kept my apartment clean, and only brought one girl - my Taiwan steady - home every couple of weeks, when I wasn't with her in Taipei.

Though six souls now inhabited the Yeh house, that number rose to seven counting the ghost of Yeh Kun-fu, great grandfather's ghost. It was with the family patriarch that I shared the fourth floor, since much of the level was devoted to honoring his memory. His shrine room was an elaborate place of worship indeed; a high and ornately carved teakwood altar took up the whole of the eastern wall, and on this beautiful piece of furniture rested a number of items. There was a large copper brazier for burning incense in the center, while a larger than life brass bust of the man himself rested off to one side. On one wall hung a photograph of great grandfather contained in a gilded frame. Wedged between the altar and the wall stood an expensive looking armoire housing incense, various items for ceremonial use, and Yeh Kun-fu's yearly allowance of *ghost money* - a scented paper currency that, at regular intervals, would be burned and sent into the heavens, presumably for spending or investing at the spirit's discretion.

With windows that looked out to a meticulously sculpted rooftop garden and out over neighboring roofs into the hills, the fourth floor was the most beautiful level of the house. But it was never used for socializing, and was seldom visited for long. Each day, grandfather would come up around dawn to light incense and place fresh fruit before his father's photograph. Mother Yeh would come up a few times a week to sweep the dark red tiled floors, bringing the vacuum up a few times a month to suck cold ash from the brazier. Other than these visits, and on certain holidays when the whole family would gather around the shrine and make their individual offerings, the fourth floor belonged only to me and great grandfather Yeh.

The patriarch and I had a comfortable arrangement. I never sensed him wandering into my half of the floor, and more importantly, neither did my girlfriend (who, being superstitious about the ghosts of other families, avoided the shrine area entirely). In turn, I kept my music low, and eventually got into the habit of making small offerings of my own - a fruit here, some nuts there. One time I stopped in the duty free shop on the way home from a visa trip to Manila and bought a box of good Cuban cigars. By that time I'd learned enough Chinese to facilitate basic communication, and so I asked Yeh Hsiao-lu if he thought his grandfather would like one of them. He told me he'd never known his grandfather to smoke cigars in life, but he might like to try one now. That night I put one of the cigars on the shrine. It was gone the next day, and I assumed that Mother Yeh had disapproved of the offering. A few days later I caught Hsiao-lu out on the balcony, smoking the cigar I'd left on the altar. He'd just closed a big deal and wanted something to celebrate it with. But he assured me his grandfather had appreciated my gesture. ❖

# Money Comes to Hakka Town

The sign on the road reads Shuangxi Tsun - Twin Streams Village. Children run through the streets while old women sell meat-filled buns in front of the town's main temple. Auntie Yeh sells betel nut, joking with the customers, enlisting friends and relatives alike to assist in the capital cranking business that is Taiwan's grassroots stock in trade. I have found myself more than once with a butter knife in one hand, huddled over a bowl filled with the semi-narcotic nuts, filling the slits with the red paste that keeps the taxi drivers going. This is the place I call home, and the people who live here are the salt of the earth.

More than that, they are the proverbial meek now inheriting the earth, or at least this part of it. Though they couldn't have known it at the time, the Hakka founders of Shuangxi had the good fortune to settle down the hill from what would one day become Taiwan's own Gleaming City on a Hill, the Hsinchu Science-Based Industrial Park. Over the last decade, the land owned by their descendants has become the most valuable in Taiwan.

Where papayas once grew, a new crop now sprouts up - huge modern apartment buildings, each of which boasts a living capacity the town founders couldn't have imagined. Soon the elevators will be turned on and the fire inspectors will be paid off. Then the outsiders will pour in, thousands upon thousands of secretaries, engineers and mid-level executives with jobs in the Science Park up the hill where so much of the world's technological wonders are made. The town will swell, and the mom and pop markets that line the village's one main street won't be able to handle the business. A brand new three-story supermarket will have to be built, and the street itself will need to be torn up and widened. The moms and pops will be handsomely compensated with stacks of thousand dollar bills, each with the identical likeness of Chiang Kai-shek beaming at them, a father figure with a smile that never fades. But will their happiness endure as their small town life is paved over? Can culture survive the onslaught of progress? ❖

(This essay was written in 1997. Many of the predictions made have come to pass.)

# Eventually It Will Rain

Somewhere on the outskirts of the southern central mountain range, it occurs to me that I am lost. My original intention was to circle around Route 23 on my rented scooter in the hopes that it would meet up with another road that might lead me back through the mountains and into Taitung City. The land is beautiful and lush, sweeping valleys filled with rice paddies and fruit trees, with green mountains on both sides. The scene is marred only by ominous black clouds moving in from over the mountains to the east. The Pacific side of Taiwan is often anything but. I stop at a small store in a ten-building town.

"Does this road lead to Taitung?" I ask the elderly proprietor sitting on the porch, lazily stroking a hound that looks not much younger.

"Don't know," he answers, his Mandarin choppy. "I've never taken it that far."

From the old man's tone and mien, I realize quickly that he is not a descendent of the Han, but of an older race to this island. Perhaps he is an Atayal, pushed down from the middle mountain range during the building of the great (and now impassable) cross island highway. More likely, he belongs to the Ami tribe who lay historical claim to this land on the far eastern edge of the island. The aboriginal population of Taiwan, like aboriginal populations nearly everywhere, did not have an easy time of it in the last few centuries. They were pushed from the fertile plains into the hills by the Hakkas, and then pushed from the hills into the mountains when the Han from Fukien pushed the Hakkas into the hills. This old man seems unperturbed, though, living in what can only be described as pretty sweet surroundings, encircled by green hills, chickens, ducks, sugarcane fields and trees bearing mangos. If not for its inaccessibility, the Hans might have pushed the natives all the way into the ocean, and the area might look like downtown Kaoshuing. But the days of wanton pushing and forced exodus are behind the old man now. As far as he seems to be concerned, all roads that matter lead to this place. I want to make conversation with him, but seem to lack the words.

"Think it'll rain?" I ask.

"Eventually," he answers most sagaciously.

As he speaks the wind kicks up, and dark clouds begin swallowing the blue sky. That and the old man's words seem to be telling me, and not in too gentle a way, that I should get back to Taitung with all due haste. ❖

# Shake, Rattle and Roll

I was sitting in my eighth floor apartment in New Garden City (NGC) mid-afternoon on a sunny Sunday, typing away and drinking my Earl Grey, when the whole place started to shake. Earthquake! I'd become inured to quakes of the *wum wum wum wum wum wum* variety, which usually caused my 25 year old building to wave gently from side to side like a tall stalk of bamboo. But this one was different, not *wum wum wum wum wum wum*, but *thump thump thump thung thump thung thump thung*, accompanied by a more pronounced vertical jack hammering of the building, with *thungs* and *thumps* punctuated by the crashing sounds of my potted plants falling over, once-precariously perched computer speakers hitting the tile floor of my home office, wind chimes jangling far beyond the call of duty, and other various and sundry clanging noises. The whole thing lasted longer than it should have, at least by my count, and when it was over, the only sounds I could hear were car alarms going off from the village eight stories below, and my own heartbeat.

Finding religion is not an uncommon reaction in these situations, and I wasn't about to waste any time by trying to think outside of the box. I heard myself moaning, "Oh sweet Jesus! Jesus! Oh sweet Jesus!" but quickly realized that after three decades of alternating between ignoring and mocking adherents of that faith, I might be barking up the wrong tree. Since

Taiwan is clearly in Buddhist hands, I quickly switched spiritual tacks, instead invoking the Chinese name of the merciful Buddha - "*Amitofo... Amitofo... Amitofo... Amitofo...*"

As I chanted, my cat emerged from her hiding place. She was an extremely pregnant stray I'd picked up off the streets weeks before, and her heavy belly nearly touched the floor. She looked up at me as I propped myself in the door frame and mewed quizzically. Soon the thumping sounds had abated, replaced by the loud jabbering from my neighbors, now running from their buildings and into the street to wait out any aftershocks. The quake had lasted as long as the one that did so much terrible damage to both the island and the collective psyche of Taiwan in September of 1999, and the people of New Garden City, spared in that one, were taking no chances. I threw my passport, laptop and camera into my bag, and made to grab the cat, but when I turned around, she was nowhere to be found. Her hiding place was vacant, and when she didn't respond to my call, I gave up on finding her and headed outside.

Despite the long jolt, there didn't seem to be any real structural damage to be seen in New Garden City. I spent the rest of the day with a bunch of other NGC residents on a large open lawn, drinking tea and listening to a portable radio. The quake had been centered in the ocean off Ilan; the only Taipei casualties had been a worker who'd fallen off a scaffolding and a taxi driver whose car had been crushed by falling construction debris. The crowd on the lawn started thinning out around sunset, and figuring the building was in no imminent danger of collapse, I headed back up to the nest.

I returned to find my apartment the same as I'd left it hours earlier, save for one difference - it was distinctly more populated by a factor of seven. The exhausted mother and her litter of seven kittens lay together in a cardboard box on the floor, stirring slightly but seemingly unshaken. ❖

# Teaching Tales

One of the good things about Taiwan is that anyone with a Western mien can get a job as an English teacher. Having even the vaguest shred of a degree helps (even if it's in underwater basket weaving), as does actually being able to speak English; however, neither of these factors is totally necessary. This ease of employment, however, can be a double edged sword - although teaching in Taiwan can offer a relatively lucrative and comfortable life, it can become somewhat of a gilded trap. Though not about teaching per se, the following stories are from the period during which I taught English in schools big and small, mostly in the city of Hsinchu.

# The Unhappy Affair at Happy Kids Kindergarten

Happy Kids American Kindergarten was the best school I'd ever worked for, so it was a shame to get arrested so early in my tenure. One moment I was sitting on a cheerfully colored pastel foam-rubber mat reading Dr. Seuss to the children, and the next I was in the back of an unmarked police car. I had first sensed something was amiss when I peered over a hardbound copy of *Green Eggs and Ham* and saw the beady eyes of an unknown man staring accusingly through the classroom window. The door opened, and Mrs. Tsai, the school principal, stepped in looking rather nervous. A gentleman needed to speak to me, she said, and the conclusion of the saga of Sam-I-Am would have to wait.

I'd been a semi-illegal but gainfully employed children's English teacher for two years, working for various kiddy schools around the city of Hsinchu. Due to the bureaucratic vagaries of Taiwanese employment laws, actually getting a working permit proved more trouble than it was worth, and while I'd heard about other Westerners getting into trouble, I'd never known anyone who'd actually been busted. The general consensus was that despite strict laws against hiring foreigners illegally, the native English teacher was a valuable commodity, good for helping Taiwan to maintain an international edge.

Usually a combination of regular visa trips on the part of the teacher and minor bribery on the part of the school sufficed to avoid any real trouble. Apparently though, my luck had run out. I looked over at the principal with a look I hoped conveyed the sentiment, 'I thought you said you had friends in the police department?' and she looked back at me with one I took to mean, 'So did I.'

Looking like a cross between Bruce Lee and Barney Fife, the plainclothes officer flashed his badge and in clipped, precise English told me, "You are breaking the law of the Republic of China. You will now be deported." He seemed quite certain of himself. Officer Fife then hustled me into an awaiting unmarked car where two of my colleagues sat nervously. As we were being driven to the police station, one of them took out a pen and surreptitiously wrote a word on his palm and flashed it quickly around. We had our group legal defense all worked out. We would play the missionary card, and plead 'Mormon.'

Something about the circumstances of our arrest was odd; for one thing, we weren't brought to the main police station, but to a smaller outlying satellite precinct. And for another, the only cop processing us was Officer Fife. The other officers seemed wholly perplexed by the situation. An hour into the interrogation, we were all sticking to our stories. Officer Fife, who initially had taken to his task with an officious glee, was now nearly apoplectic.

"Why are you wasting my time? I do not believe that you are all Mormons, teaching children for love and not money. You are all illegal teachers, and you will all be deported from the

Republic of China."

Somewhere during the second hour an older and better dressed inspector entered and spoke to Officer Fife. The older officer addressed him in Hakka. Hsinchu is a Hakka city, and most Hsinchu cops can speak the dialect. Officer Fife, however, couldn't understand a word of Hakka, so the older officer switched to Mandarin. Though I barely spoke Mandarin at the time, I noticed that the words 'wrong' and 'foreigner' kept coming up.

The older cop left, and Officer Fife turned to us, looking both angry and embarrassed. "We are keeping your passports until…um…until our investigations are complete." He was now fishing for the proper English, seeming less certain of himself by the minute. "You are, ah, free to go now. We will, ah, call you when we have made our…decision."

I returned to the school to pick up my motorcycle, still parked out front. Though well past class hours, the lights were still on inside. Principal Tsai came out as soon as she saw me. She looked very sad.

"We do not understand what has happened! We have friends in the Hsinchu police. They told us that they would always call us first if they had to come to check for illegal workers. We called our friends, and they didn't know what was going on except that the policeman who arrested you was not one of theirs. They think that some other school has friends in the police in another county, and are trying to scare us."

I spent the next three days wondering whether or not to pack. On the fourth day, Miss Yeh, my landlady, told me that the police had called, and that I was to appear that afternoon at the station, not at the smaller precinct we'd been brought to, but the main station downtown.

When I got there, Officer Fife was nowhere to be seen. Instead, the older inspector was sitting in an office with another plainclothes officer. My passport was sitting on the desk. The plainclothes officer addressed me in English.

"We are sorry for the inconvenience, Mr. Brown. After reviewing the situation, we have determined that you have done nothing wrong." He pushed my passport towards me.

"Please feel welcome to continue your life in Hsinchu," he said, walking me to the door.

I left, relieved and perplexed. When I met up with the other teachers at a coffee shop later that evening, we agreed that the whole affair had botched vendetta written all over it. Beyond that, we had no idea what had transpired. Though Principal Tsai promised us that the incident wouldn't be repeated, we were all too freaked out to return to a marked school, and found different jobs. And Happy Kids? Marked as hot, and unable to attract more foreign teachers, the school soon closed down, another unhappy victim of the cutthroat politics of the world of Taiwanese kindergartens. ❖

# Mister Happy Gets His

Nobody liked Happy. The head teacher at an overpriced English kindergarten rumored to be owned by the Kuomintang, Happy was married to the best friend of the school's owner and ran the place like a personal fiefdom. Among the Hsinchu English teacher circuit, Happy had a reputation for hiring and firing on a whim, and for being a complete prick in general. He was pale, skinny and wore a scraggly mustache and crooked grin, as if to say to those working under him, "Eat shit. I'm sleeping with your employer's best friend." But the most infuriating thing about Happy was that everyone who knew him had to call him Happy. Nobody knew his real name; even the business cards he handed to casual acquaintances read 'Mr. Happy, English Teacher.'

Zippo was another local foreigner with an unusual name, but he was cut from a different cloth entirely. Attached to no school in particular, Zippo had earned a reputation as one of the best children's teachers in town. Happy had hired Zippo at the beginning of the summer rush, when classes fill up suddenly and foreign teachers are in short supply. To say that Happy disliked Zippo would be an understatement; Zippo was competent and well liked by students and fellow teachers. Happy knew that he was neither of these, and saw in Zippo the man he could never be. Predictably, Happy fired Zippo as soon as he found a suitable replacement, using as a vague excuse that one of the students had complained that Zippo had been too strict. Zippo was upset, because he liked his kids, but he wasn't surprised. He knew when he signed up that those who became too well-liked never lasted long in Happy's kingdom.

"Guys like Happy always get theirs in the end," Zippo would later say. "Mark my words."

In Happy's case, come-uppance wasn't long in coming. That autumn, word came through the local foreigner grapevine that the KMT kindergarten was looking for a new head teacher. Details were vague at first, but rumors soon circulated concerning a terrible falling out between Happy's wife and her once-best friend, leading to very bad blood between Happy and his patron. A secretary working in the office claimed to have witnessed a particularly nasty row in which Happy had flipped out and called his employer a bitch. And this, according to the secretary, was only for starters.

'Bitch' is the one pejorative not hurled lightly in Taiwan, especially not at one's boss. The secretary had no way of knowing if Happy was surprised when his boss reacted with an open-handed slap to Happy's face that was so loud it could be heard out in the playground. But it's likely that the boss was shocked by Happy's response.

He slapped her back.

The details of what happened next are sketchy. Those who had worked for Happy knew him as an officious and generally odious individual, but nobody had ever accused him of being suicidal. And one thing no sane foreigner living in Taiwan should ever do, even in the heat of argument, is to slap the

*Mister Happy Gets His*

wife of a mid-ranking Kuomintang official. It is entirely possible that immediately after striking his boss, Happy had a moment of chilling clarity. Enmity between his family and that of the boss of the Kuomintang kindergarten sealed, he left in haste, not even returning to pick up his last paycheck.

But the wife of a Kuomintang official does not easily forget the ignominy of being struck by an employee. And hell hath no fury like that of an angry woman with political clout. After hiring a new head teacher, she put out her feelers, and within a few weeks the principal learned that Happy had gotten a job teaching at another kindergarten on the other side of town. Though the Hsinchu police department was too large and professional for her husband to exert any leverage, she was able to convince him to make a call to certain officials working in a smaller city nearby.

The next week, an English speaking policeman posing as a local foreign affairs officer, drove into Hsinchu with the mission of visiting Happy's new place of employment, and arresting him for teaching on a lapsed work visa. As the officer was well out of his jurisdiction, he wouldn't be able to actually enforce anything, but the principal was sure that the harassment would send a message to Happy. Leave town, while you still can.

But the out-of-town cop didn't know exactly which school Happy worked at, only which neighborhood it was in. He entered the first English kindergarten he passed, and after flashing his badge and bullying his way past the Taiwanese staff, he found that it was staffed by not one but three foreign teachers. After rousting them away from their classes, he checked their passports, realizing too late that it was unlikely that his target's legal name would actually be Happy.

Confused, but no less determined to get into the good graces of his high-ranking Kuomintang friend, he dragged all of the foreigners on the premises to a small satellite precinct on the edge of town where he hoped to determine, through rigorous police methodology, which of the bunch was the notorious Happy.

Unfortunately for all involved, the out-of-town cop had gone to the wrong school. It took intervention by the chief officer of the Hsinchu foreign affairs police (whose position, and understandably so, was that he was the only arbiter on which of the city's many illegal English schools would be shut down and when) to clear the confusion. The out-of-town cop was sent home, and the three American teachers were freed from custody.

Word of the incident quickly got around the local English teacher community, and eventually Happy got the message that he was no longer welcome in Hsinchu. Some people say that he and his wife moved to Taipei and opened up their own school, while others claim that he packed it in and moved back to the States. But nobody was sorry to learn he was gone. Nobody liked Happy. ✤

# Skinny Asses

"Look at this," my friend Jo-an said, shaking her ample derrière in my direction. "How can I compete with all the skinny asses with this thing sticking out of me?" Jo's ass was big, but beautifully shaped. She had curves up front to match too; with her figure, she'd have had men falling at her feet from Moscow to Lisbon, New York to Compton. But in Taiwan, Jo's statuesque physique was just another strike against her in the local dating market.

"I haven't had a date in almost a year," Jo continued. "Your average Taiwanese guy is either totally turned off by the size of my ass…"

"Or totally turned on, but too much of a mamma's boy to ask you out."

"I was getting to that, exactly. Or they're married. And you Western men…"

"…don't get me involved in this."

"Don't interrupt! You Western men are all like slobs at a smorgasbord, with all those hot Taiwanese chicks fawning over you everywhere you go. Hot commodities, you all are, and you know it. So you pick and choose, pick and choose! It's disgusting."

"You mean, like attractive women back in the West?"

"Exactly. And that's the way it ought to be."

Jo's complaint was common among expatriate women living in Taiwan. A dearth of Taiwanese men who were interested - or able to act on any interest they might have - in Western women effectively shrunk the dating pool by about 98%. And as for the other two percent, she wasn't wrong - foreign men were a hot commodity. This created a palpable frustration among single foreign women living in Taiwan, which they often vented in the presence of their male friends.

"It's like a wet-dream come true for you guys…all these fawning, obedient Asian babes hanging all over you."

"Obedient, eh?" I asked, raising an eyebrow. "And where did you hear that?"

"Oh, come on!" she said, giving me an eyebrow raise of her own. "Everybody knows that Asian women are all like, 'OK hon-ee, whatever you want, everything up to boy friend!'"

Jo put one hand on her hip and another behind her head, making a mincing gesture.

"Look, I hate to burst your self-pity bubble, but that stereotype just isn't true. I've only been with two Taiwanese women, and both were long term things - and neither one was anything but an equal partner in the relationship. Have you considered the fact that just maybe the reason that so many Western men come to Taiwan and wind up hitched is that Taiwanese women are actually looking for meaningful partnerships, while Western women set their standards incredibly high and play too many damned games?"

Jo snorted loudly.

"So you mean that Western women are just into game playing, huh?"

"Hey, you admitted it already. Back home if a woman is hot, she thinks she can play with one guy's affection until she gets bored, then drop him when someone she thinks is better comes along. In my experience, most Taiwanese women aren't like this. They're more loyal, less….superficial."

"Yeah, right…" her voice was bitter. "I think you're just like all the rest of the foreign guys living here. You all have yellow fever."

"Yellow fever" is a derogatory description for a man who only goes for Asian women. As far as I'm concerned, it's a conversation ender.

"Look Jo, that's just racist. Sorry you aren't getting laid, but I have to prepare for class."

I left Jo to stew in her estrogen and went off to teach. Later that week I ran into her, and the incident was forgotten. We had a cup of coffee and made small talk about the news of the day. The Clinton / Lewinsky scandal was making headlines, even in Taiwan.

"At least Monica's getting laid," Jo commented.

"I'm not sure that counts as getting laid," I answered.

A couple of months later, the school got a new teacher, Phil, a Canadian guy. Short, in his mid thirties, Phil was a bit older than your average adult conversation school teacher. But he had all his hair and was an amiable enough guy. Most importantly to Jo, he was new in Taiwan, seemingly heterosexual, and unattached. Predictably, Jo was on him the week he arrived. They wound up going out for a little while, and the girls behind the counter at the school were already making jokes about the two being a couple. Their relationship, though, didn't last more than a couple of months. At first I assumed that Phil had realized that he was a far hotter property on the dating scene than he'd been back home in Canada and broken it off. But it turns out that Jo had dumped Phil.

"So why did you break it off with Phil?" I asked her a few weeks after it had ended. "He seemed like a good enough guy."

"Eh..." she answered half-heartedly. "I prefer taller men." ❖

# Bless the Beasts and Pass the Betel Nut

I rise with the dust cloud, when the radioactive particles crawl up my nose and pry their way under my eyelids. This is my alarm clock. I sneeze for 30 minutes each morning. The earth seeps inside me during the night, and I atomize it every morning. I am a link between earth and sky.

In the mornings, I teach English to pre-school children. I must be chipper. I am an ambassador. This morning the children were rough on me. Very rough. They began taunting me early, and my eyes darted around the room, desperate for help of any kind.

It was not to come. The assistant they assigned me was sitting on her heels, rocking back and forth and smiling contentedly. Utterly useless.

Several of the children were circling me, a few of them making quick leaps in my direction, which I easily fended off. But they had the staying power of youth, and I am so old. How long could I hold out?

I decided not to find out.

"Hordes of Beelzebub, sit thee down!" I screamed, tearing off my shirt to reveal the tattoo of the leering, pipe-smoking man known as BOB that resides on my left arm. "Do you want to meet BOB?"

At the mention of BOB the little ones grew quiet. A few of the smaller ones began weeping.

"You remember BOB, don't you?"

Of course, the children, not understanding English, heard my words as meaningless gibberish. But they understood the wrath of BOB only too well. I did a slow scan of the room, taking care to make eye contact with the beasts.

"Just get back into your little chairs, nice and slow, and everybody gets home tonight, nice and safe."

That seemed to scare them. That is, all except one. I had grown overconfident, and turned my back on them. By the time I realized my mistake, it was too late.

She was a big one. Five, maybe five and a half. Thirty-five pounds of terror, coming at me like a bone crushing juggernaut straight from the darkest pits of hell. This was a tyke out for blood, and I knew it would take more than the threat of BOB to stop her now. This time it was for real.

"Come and shake hands with BOB!" I screamed, half out of my mind with adrenalin spawned terror.

She had a rolled up book in her hand, and was out for more than just a playful slap. I grappled with her for an eternity, while the rest of the class screamed, "*Da pang zhu laoshi*" -

"Teacher is a big fat pig." Too late, I realized that this had been their plan all along. Send the oldest among them to engage me physically while the rest tormented me mentally - a ruthless, cunning plan, the sort of which only Taiwanese preschoolers could conceive.

The unspeakably cute child was using every one of her thirty-five pounds to crush my bones into powder. I felt myself losing consciousness.

"BOB..." I gasped, "...don't let it end this way..."

There was a sound - gunfire perhaps, or an explosion? Had the president called in an air strike on my behalf?

No, it was a bell. The death grip of the indescribably adorable five year old slackened and released, as she, along with the rest of her satanic coven, ran out of the room for cookies.

Heaving a sigh of relief, I walked out. The Chinese assistant said something to me like, "Oh, your Chinese is getting very good."

But I wasn't listening. I was already half way out of the room, dreaming about being halfway to the bottom of a bowl of trail mix made with cheap Taiwanese tranquilizers, betel nuts, and nicotine patches. ❖

(Note: In the mid 1990s, a group of expatriates began publishing a small, literary magazine called *The New Expatriate*. Though *TNE* only lasted a few years, it proved a much welcome home for some of my more experimental prose, a category into which this story definitely fits. And yes, I swear...it's pure fiction.)

# Stories About People

Taiwan is an island of roughly 21 million people, or to be more descriptive, 21 million characters. The following stories concern people I know, have known, or at the very least, know of.

# Humble Mahjong Loser

Mr. Su was no failure. Anything but. Not only did he own the largest grocery store in the Central Taiwan mountain town of Tsaotun (offering eight aisles, including a full walk-in refrigerated case in the back and produce bins out in front), but he didn't even have to get his hands dirty doing any of the heavy work required to keep the market going. He'd hired a girl to sit behind the front counter; her only job was to look pretty and take money from customers. And he'd hired a boy, seventeen maybe, not the sharpest tool in the shed but a good lifter. The boy's job was to make sure that the aisles were always stocked, that the packages of dried noodles and canned squid in black-bean sauce were always priced (slightly higher maybe than the same product might cost down in the big city, but the shop brought such convenience to the small town), and that the produce was always fresh, or at least looked that way.

And he had a wife; this was important because it meant that Mr. Su didn't even have to do any of the actual heavy lifting of management, that is to say, to make sure that the help did their jobs right. The boy (again, none too bright) needed to be told that if he mixed up the prices of canned abalone and tuna one more time, the difference would come out of his pay, and the girl needed to be reminded that she wasn't fooling anybody by having her no-good scooter thug boyfriend come in late at night pretending to be a customer. The walls had eyes, the wife would tell her, and the boy had a bad reputation, and besides, she was at heart a nice girl who could do much better. So Mr. Su, freed from having to actually run the store which he legally owned, could concentrate on his true love - playing mahjong.

Mr. Su was an extremely skilled player, the best in town according to many. And Tsaotun was hardly some kind of one-horse town in which being the most skilled mahjong player meant nothing. Though hardly a metropolis, it was still, after all, Taiwan, an island no bigger than New Jersey with a population twice that of the greater tri-state area. Even a small town like Tsaotun had at least twenty-five thousand people, and among these a goodly number were skilled gamblers. So to say that Mr. Su was said to be the best in town (even a small sized town like Tsaotun) was nothing to sneeze at.

Mr. Su owned the apartment above the store, but he didn't rent it out. It was a small place with bare concrete walls, tiled floors, a bedroom (in which empty boxes from the store were kept, pending weekly visits from the man from the cardboard recyclers), a kitchen and a bathroom. The only furniture consisted of four wooden chairs and a beautiful mahjong table, ornately carved from a hunk of imported redwood with a soft felt overlay that both minimized the clacking and assured the smooth shuffling of tiles. On most nights and some days, Mr. Su could be found here playing mahjong, while downstairs, his wife went about making sure that the store continued turning a profit.

And what did his wife think? She reasoned that her husband's gambling was not necessarily a bad thing, because it meant that she always knew where he was. The muffled plastic clacking of shuffling tiles was a constant reminder that her husband was just a few yards above her head, and not off in the city spending their hard-earned money chasing karaoke parlor girls (as did the husbands of so many of her long-suffering friends). Also, she knew he was a skilled player (the best in town, many said) and more often than not he came out ahead or at least not too far behind. So she accepted his gambling, telling herself that, as husbands went, she could be much worse off.

Mr. Su's reputation as a skilled gambler reached the towns further down the mountain, and eventually into the big city of Taichung. This reputation drew small time punters up from the city, men who didn't mind making the 45 minute drive up into the mountains in order to test their skill against a local legend. City players brought city money, and the stakes grew increasingly larger, until the only local player who could afford to stay in the game was Mr. Su himself. For a few weeks, Mr. Su's wealth grew as he played, and won, stakes that would have been impossible to get local players to raise, let alone gamble. Things were going so well for Mr. Su that he rented a local restaurant to throw a party during the Mid-Autumn Festival. Friends and family came from as far away as Pingtung and Miaoli to feast on drunken chicken, sautéed oysters in black bean sauce, deep fried prawn, shark's fin stew with abalone, and scores of other traditional Taiwanese dishes that everyone agreed were not merely the best quality, but also the most expensive available. Mr. Su continued winning through the autumn. But in the winter, it all came crashing down.

People in Tsaotun to this day speak in awed whispers about the night that three men from the city came up to play mahjong at Mr. Su's table. These men were different, no doubt about it. Each drove a shiny white BMW, the likes of which had not been seen in town before. They parked their cars in a row before Mr. Su's supermarket. And the men who stepped out of the cars, according to those who saw them in the moments between parking and going upstairs, were dressed a caliber above even the city-people who had of late come to play with Mr. Su: sharp, wide-collared black suit jackets, creased pants, and not bare feet but socks - black, no less - inside of plastic flip-flops.

On the night they came, Mrs. Su sent the help home earlier than usual, after going upstairs to bring the men more sandwiches and sunflower seeds. Her husband hadn't touched the one she'd brought up hours earlier, and looked even more distracted than he usually did. He told her not to wait up for him. She went downstairs and closed up the shop, paid the boy and girl their salaries, which weren't actually due until the next day, then sent them home. She walked through the store one more time, making sure that everything was in order for the next day, that the coolers were all turned down to the lowest practical setting, and finally, perhaps overcome by a foreboding sense of nostalgia, she swept the floor one last time before closing the lights and shuttering the shop. As she walked out into the cold, early winter mountain air, she could still hear the clacking of tiles as she walked down the darkened streets.

In the morning it was gone - the register and the cash within, the cooler along with the dairy products, the produce, the cans of abalone, squid and tuna, and the store itself. Of course, the store was still physically there, as were all of the items within, save the cash left in the register. But in reality, the Su family's store was gone as surely as if it had been vaporized. She'd awoken as the sun was coming up to the sound of her husband rifling through a filing cabinet in the living room of their home, and when she got out of bed she found he was gone, along with the keys to the padlock that secured the store's metal gate. Though she knew in her heart that something terrible had happened, she walked over to the store anyway, to open it at seven as she always did, though today she had no keys. The shiny white BMW cars were gone, leaving nothing but a set of black tire marks where one had pulled out too quickly. She didn't bang on the gates; she didn't need to. Instead, she went upstairs to find her husband, arms splayed across the scattered tiles on the handsome wooden table like a dead man floating in a shallow pond, face pressed against the crushed green velvet, sobbing softly. Without saying a word, she walked home and began packing.

They let him keep working in the store, the men who now owned it. Every week they would send someone up from the city to collect their profits, make sure that the bookkeeping was being done properly, and pay Mr. Su a salary that, all agreed, was generous under the circumstances. After the house was sold, Mr. Su moved into the apartment above the store, putting a small cot in the corner of the room used to store the cardboard boxes. The girl, being both pretty and good-hearted, found a job at a grocery store in the next town. The boy stuck around for a few weeks out of loyalty before being called up to do his mandatory army service. And his wife? She was never seen in Tsaotun again. Rumor had it that she'd moved back to live with her family in Pingtung, and that she'd craftily kept the house they'd shared in her name, and was able to sell it through a proxy at not too great a loss. The house had been a wedding gift from her father; the beautifully handcrafted wooden mahjong table, now gathering dust in the center of the apartment above the grocery store, had been a gift from his. ❖

# Betel Nut Ingénue

*Binglan xiaojiemen (betel nut girls) are ubiquitous in cities and towns throughout Taiwan. These scantily clad women sit on the side of the road in transparent glass booths, from which they dispense baggies of betel nut, a mildly narcotic locally grown substance ingested primarily by men, usually taxi drivers, truckers and so forth. Though every so often some government official looking to score points with the high-minded morality crowd will lead a crusade to get betel nuts banned (or at least to get betel nut girls to dress more modestly), little has come from these efforts. This story was inspired by a friend of mine who spent time getting to know some of these women. The first words, meaning 'tell me', are in the Taiwanese dialect.*

"*Ga wu gong-a!*" Ah-wei laughed, slapping Ah-nei's bare white shoulder with her palm. "Was it romantic? I hear foreigner men are so romantic. Tell me! Tell me!"

"Hmmmm...let me think." Ah-nei ran long fingers through her hair as if trying to conjure up moments past, prolonging her friend's suspense. "Yes, definitely."

"Lucky! I can't stand you!"

A blue Hyundai announced itself before the glass booth, tires

crunching on gravel. "This one is mine." Ah-nei grabbed two baggies of betel nut and walked to the car, flamingo-like on high heels. Ah-nei bent down at the waist and presented the driver with a full view of the goods offered and those about which he could only dream.

"Two bags leaf-wrapped, right handsome?"

The driver was in his early forties by the looks of him; he'd bought from the stand a few times before, always on Monday mornings. He was, by the looks of his car, a family man, and Ah-nei assumed he was a businessman. The small struggles and low-grade disappointments of his life were just beginning to etch their map on the skin of his face. Ah-nei imagined the man leaving a doting *tai-tai* at home in a big apartment in Ilan on Monday mornings, leaving her to raise their child in a healthier environment while he drove into Taipei to manage whatever his business was during the week. She imagined that he had a small, non-descript efficiency apartment somewhere in Taipei not far from the office; he tried to drive back at least once or twice mid-week to spend the night with his wife and child. He loved his wife, or so he told himself, but couldn't deny that he felt as if he'd compromised somewhere along the line. These thoughts he dealt with through drink, and the occasional debauch. Though she did not know his name, Ah-nei knew that she represented to him just a small taste of the latter. She smiled inwardly at the realization that in some small way she had a place in the envi-

# The Fruit Lady of Shita

In the afternoon she opens shop, chopping mangos, papayas, cantaloupe, honeydew melons, strawberries, along with various other esoteric Taiwanese fruits, and laying the chunks out on blocks of ice. In the hours before sunset, her customer base is comprised mainly of students from the nearby university. When the sun goes down, the fruit lady sells plastic bags filled with chopped fruit to people from all walks of Taipei life, from taxi drivers to well dressed executives, mid-level salary men to inebriated foreign students out on the town. She's perpetually merry and bright, offering free samples to all takers and never batting an eye.

For years, I knew her only as the fruit lady, having never learned her proper name despite the fact that she's long been among my favorite people in Taipei. Face to face I address her as *Jie-jie*, or older sister, which infuriates her as she's only a year older than me. But I'm not comfortable calling her *Mei-mei*, or younger sister; it sounds flirtatious, and she's a married woman. Her stand occupies a prime chunk of corner real estate in the outdoor food market on the south end of Shita University.

Strangely enough, our first conversation ended in an argument. I don't remember the details exactly, a misunderstanding probably, mistaken communication between a native and newly-studied student of Mandarin both having bad days. But her fruit was some of the best to be found in Taipei, and though I initially returned for the fruit, as my Mandarin improved, I found myself increasingly drawn into lengthy conversations with my fruit lady. At first our conversations mostly consisted of her questions and my answers. Queries about salary, over chunks of honeydew. What about my girlfriend, and did her parents know their daughter had a Westerner, over strawberries.

Perhaps it was because my Mandarin improved, or maybe it was because the relationship had just progressed, but before long my fruit lady was telling me things about herself. She was from down south, but came to Taipei with her identical twin sister to open up shops. Her twin had also opened up a fruit stand, in a night market across town. She had two daughters, and was concerned because they didn't seem to enjoy studying English. She wanted to travel, but was too busy making money to think about anything but business. When the children were a bit older, she thought she and her husband might do some traveling, but that was a long way off yet. Eventually, she stopped taking money from me altogether, and any time I came by, she would give me a clear plastic bag stuffed full of assorted fruit chunks for which a regular customer might have paid 200 NT. She refused to take my money no matter what I said, and still does to this day.

The one topic my fruit lady had always been reticent to discuss with me was politics, usually a hot button topic among Taiwanese. Recently, I found myself chatting with her in the early evening hours following a massive rally held in response to Beijing's anti-secession law. It had been the largest political rally in years, and I thought that with emotions still running high and the market unusually crowded with marchers filtering from the rally, I might be able to draw her out.

"Surely, you must have some feelings about which party has Taiwan's best interest in mind," I ventured. She just laughed.

"Nationalist party...New Party...Democratic Progressive Party," she laughed, going down the list of prominent Taiwanese political factions. "I belong to the 'Me Party.' I'm the only member, and my platform is get on with my business."

A group of bedraggled looking marchers passed by, all wearing green caps bearing the DPP logo. "Taiwan Independence," one of them yelled, and my friend smiled and handed him a toothpick with a chunk of melon on the end. Though it didn't happen, I believe that had a second group wearing caps with Kuomintang logos passed ten minutes later, shouting, "Long live one China!" my friend the fruit lady would have done the same, never batting an eye. ❖

# The Master Has Fast Hands

My friend Kyle had been trying to get me to come down to the Shita University neighborhood for months to watch him spar with his new martial arts sensei. Eventually I gave in and called him up. "Where's the dojo?" I asked.

"It's kind of a floating thing," Kyle answered. "Master Szeto doesn't believe in keeping himself anchored down to one place. His dojo travels with him."

In other words, Master Szeto is kind of a gypsy teacher, who, lacking his own place, set up his classes at the convenience of his students, usually in parks.

This evening's lesson is slated for sundown on the Shita campus. Kyle is there, along with three other students, and of course the master himself. I watch as he and his students engage in what at first looked not so much like traditional Kung Fu, but a well orchestrated slap-boxing match. Wing Chun Kuen is a style that does not fit into most people's concept of what Kung Fu looks like, despite the fact that Wing Chun is the system that Bruce Lee cut his teeth on. But a few moments of observation tells me that there was far more control between the combatants than met the eye.

Master Szeto speaks with me as he instructs two of his students engaging in a bout of sticky hands, a typical Wing Chun practice that resembles a cross between Tai Chi, Chi Gong, and an old fashioned slap-match. I have to admit that there was certainly a science to this martial art, as the two combatants seemed to move the energy of each other's blows and transform it into energy of their own. Indeed, unlike other martial arts that seem based on specific techniques ('blow and counterblow' and specific combinations of motions), Wing Chun is based on simple principles of movement and training.

"Wing Chun is not concerned with drama, nor is it about looking good," Master Szeto says. "Rather, Wing Chun is based on intuition, on developing the intuition of the students so that they can both maximize their own power and use the very power of their opponents against them. Observe."

After about thirty minutes of sparring between students, I'm in for a treat as Master Szeto announces that he'll now be sparring with Kyle. To be honest, the master doesn't seem to do much striking. Rather, he keeps taking blow after blow from his student and turning them away with utter economy of movement, much like a child's pinwheel redirects the wind.

"A sparring dummy is an important training tool for Wing Chun," he explains, redirecting Kyle's every blow. "As this class is being held outside, in lieu of equipment I have played the role of Kyle's sparring dummy."

At the end of this session, Kyle is covered in sweat and breathing heavily. He bows deeply, thanking Master Szeto for the opportunity, and heads for his towel. The master hasn't even broken the slightest sweat. He looks like a man who's just spent ten minutes playing with a kitten. ✣

*The Master Has Fast Hands*

# Your Friend, Khalil

When my good friend Zippo announced his plan to fly to New Delhi, buy a camel, and ride it to Morocco, I didn't bat an eye. Not because I didn't believe he didn't have the guts to do it, or at least try, and not because Zippo was not only a good fifty kilos overweight and, to my knowledge, had never so much as visited a petting zoo. The problem with Zippo's plan was more of an immediate logistical one. Though a locally beloved foreign teacher with a gift for the gab that both Taiwanese children and adult students found eminently hirable, Zippo lacked the educational background required to obtain a legal working permit. As a result, he was in the country on a tourist visa that, owing to his personal unwillingness to compromise his anti-authoritarian principles by leaving the country every 60 days (as per Taiwanese law), had expired several years ago. This meant that Zippo, unlike me, could not just take a bus to Chiang Kai-shek Airport and board an outward bound airplane, let alone hope to ever return to his life in Taiwan, a life which by his own account was comfortable, though at times a bit monotonous.

"Ignoring the fact that you've never even ridden a horse, let alone a camel," I began, "and that such a ride would take you through the most volatile and desolate regions of Central Asia, the Middle East, and then, should you last so long, North Africa…"

"I've got that all worked out. When I get to New Delhi, I'll become a Muslim, and declare that my journey is a pilgrimage of peace. I'll spend a month or two drumming up publicity through the Islamic press. Can you imagine the headline? Fat New Zealander sees the light, begins peace pilgrimage across land of Islam. Once word gets around, I'll be a celebrity in the Islamic world... people will be lining up just to help me out."

"And the money for this epic journey will come from where?"

"I've got that lined up. You remember my student Fred, one of the executives I teach at night in the science park? He said he'd pony up five thousand dollars U.S. in exchange for some publicity for his company. I was thinking I'd name the camel Fred in his honor."

"I'm sure he'll be flattered. But what about your visa? You've overstayed your 60 day visa by five years. Even if they let you out, you won't get back in."

"That's the beauty part! When I convert, I'll take a Muslim name. When the trip is done, I'll fly back to New Zealand and make it all nice and legal, dot the *i*'s and cross the *t*'s, and get a new passport with the new name. I've done that part before, mate. You don't think I was born a Zippo, do you?"

In his own clearly insane way, Zippo seemed to have thought the whole thing through. He was still a bit vague on the actual mechanics of the journey, which would involve him crossing 4000 miles of deserts, mountain ranges, and international borders. But he did have a lead on the location of the camel market in New Delhi, and this, we both felt, was the right place to start.

He actually had less of a problem than I'd anticipated in leaving the country. According to Zippo, when he turned himself in to the Hsinchu foreign affairs police, they were pretty nice to him, and gave him several cups of oolong tea during the interrogation. When they asked him why he'd overstayed his visa by five years, he told them that he'd forgotten he had to leave. As to how he'd been living all these years, he claimed to have met a rich married woman who'd only recently grown bored of him. They didn't believe him, of course, but he spoke good Taiwanese and was very polite, so after making him pay a minimal fine, they gave him 48 hours to leave and stamped "not eligible for further ROC visas" into his passport.

And so I didn't bat an eye when, a few months later, a postcard arrived:

*India was fine, but Pakistan is turning out to be more difficult than I'd thought. I have dysentery and Fred is a real pain in the ass.*

The card was postmarked Karachi and signed, Your friend, Khalil. ❖

# Journalistic Forays in Formosa

In late 2001, I returned to Taiwan after a three year hiatus, half of which was spent traveling around China and the other, living in North America. In China, I'd spent a summer working for a very hip English weekly called *Beijing Scene*, and though no similar magazine existed in Taiwan, I decided that I would endeavor to continue playing the role of cutting-edged gonzo journalist that I had started in Beijing. At the very least, I promised myself that I wouldn't fall back into the trap of English teaching…at least not full time. The following stories come from this period.

# Lantern Festival

It was the first day of the Lantern Festival in The Year of the Horse, but I had no intention of seeing the floats. I'd been in bed most of the day with a bad case of food poisoning, possibly caused by some bad dumplings. At 4:30, the bleating of my cell phone jarred me out of a sweet afternoon's delirium. It was my editor, and she wasn't interested in dumplings, poisoned or otherwise. "Today is the first day of the Lantern Festival," she reminded me. "Get down there and don't come back until you have 500 words, some photos, and the witty captions I've come to expect from you." I scraped myself off of my tatami, and hitched a ride down the mountain with a local scooter lunatic.

By the time I got to Chiang Kai-shek Park, the festivities were already in full swing, and the place was packed on all sides and everywhere in between. I headed down Aigwo West Road, attempting to make a beeline for the food stalls over by Hang Zhou S. Road, but it was tough going. The sidewalks on the south side were completely *ren shan ren hai*, a colloquial term meaning "people mountain people sea," or crowded as hell. On the north side, the pavement was packed with people and the year's lantern floats. Some of the floats were fairly self explanatory - horses, angels, that sort of thing. Others were a bit strange, even for a man of my eclectic tastes. Yulon Motors' "Marvels of the Ocean" float started off with a fairly straight forward motif of an octopus, a shark, and some fish floating in a translucent ocean.

But what was I supposed to make of the angels with Hello Kitty faces hovering above the whole mess? Luckily, my mind was distracted from this by the more straightforward "Matching Dragons," which depicted two wizened old winged lizards engaging in a life or death struggle over a game of Chinese Chess.

I made it to the food court, and got a bag of deathly sweet honeyed yams and an ear of grilled corn. This was the most I could handle, as I hadn't eaten in over a day, and the last thing I had eaten damn near killed me. There seemed to be a lot more booths hawking aboriginal goods at this year's festival, but, fortunately for me, there were no freshly slaughtered pigs - with my weakened constitution, I don't think I could have taken it. I knocked back the food with a few shot glasses of complimentary green tea, and made my way inside the park, where the festivities were officially beginning with a synchronized drum and light show centered on a gigantic horse float.

It was crowded inside the park, and I could barely move. The only direction I could really get an unobstructed view of was up, allowing me to take notice of the ten or more severed head balloons floating above the festivities. The heads belonged to cartoon characters mostly, and I know that they were strictly for the kids, but still, in my condition, the sight of gigantic dismembered heads grinning 20 feet above my own didn't sit well. I stuck around until nine to watch a few performances, and then headed back to the subway that would take me home. I'd had enough of festivities and disembodied heads to last me for a while. ❖

*Lantern Festival*

# Death by Cholesterol

Suicide in this primarily Buddhist nation is frowned upon. However, should the horrible futility of life be weighing ever heavier upon your soul, there exists one sure-fire way to ensure a painless, delicious demise - death by cholesterol, at the Shilin Night Market. As assisted suicide is illegal in Taiwan, I will couch my advice to you, my terminally depressed friend, in negative terms, advising readers inclined to continue living to stick to the lighter fare being peddled on the market's outer spokes - fried pastries, duck wings, squid-on-a-stick, and other slow killing delicacies - and not make their way into the enclosed food court that forms the Shilin Night Market's greasy innards. For starters, do not order as an appetizer three famous Taiwanese oyster pancakes - delicious fresh oysters folded into a pure egg batter and fried in lard. Following this, do not go to one of the *cho dofu* stalls and get yourself a few orders of deep fried fermented tofu served with a heaping helping of pickled vegetables and hot sauce. Finally, under no circumstances should you order a plate of "Taiwanese beefsteak." This meal, which consists of a huge slab of grade D beef fried in lard on a hot plate, slathered in gravy and served with a side of greasy spaghetti and a raw egg cracked on top, will almost certainly kill you.

Should dame fate decide that your ticket is not yet up, and somehow give your tormented cardiovascular system the

strength to pump out the pounds of grease which you, in your melancholic stupor, pumped in there, take this as a sign from the gods that your time is not as yet nigh. Under no circumstances should you attempt to finish the job by consuming half-a-dozen *da bing p'ao hsiao bing* (big cake wrapped around little cake). The fried delights, a Shilin specialty, should be enough to help you pull the plug for good. If not, cheer up; there will always be other nights. ❖

# Drought

Taiwan in spring, particularly up north, is known for its wet weather. Locals say the island has two seasons: Cold and Damp, and Hot and Wet. April, the month usually dreaded by most in Taipei for its Seattle-like dreariness, came on this year more like Tripoli in August. While coming home with dry clothes was kind of nice, something about the unnatural abundance of sunshine was downright eerie. The specter of drought looms large, and if the famous Plum Rains of spring don't come soon, Taiwan is up shit creek, and a dry creek it will be. Already there's talk of having to divert water from agriculture to run the semiconductor factories in Hsinchu, and Taiwan is facing a summer of parched rice fields, fruitless orange trees, and higher betel nut prices. And of course, I'll have to keep stealing water from my neighbors.

My little mountain community of New Garden City isn't just removed from the traffic and hustle of Taipei; it's also removed from the Feitsui Reservoir, from which much of Taipei City drinks. What we have here is a small community reservoir which is fed from a stream that runs down the mountain, itself fed from precipitation that occurs way up in the high altitudes. And this year, the dry winter and drier spring translated into water rationing. It started out innocuously enough - in mid April, the water began being shut off from noon until five, and from midnight until six. By May first, the situation got more critical as our little reservoir dipped below the dead storage mark, the level at which they actually have to pump the remaining water out. Without the pressure to carry the remaining supply up, the water in my eighth floor apartment stopped entirely. In fact, the only people past the third floor getting any water at all were those with their own personal rooftop storage tanks with built in pumps.

Lack of water also does strange things to one's mind. I've found myself opening up defunct taps and staring at them for minutes at a time, and holding down the toilet handle, as if that little bit of extra pressure might do the trick, making a tank that's been dry for weeks magically issue forth with a sweet flushing sound.

Lack of water also warps one's sense of ethics. While I haven't yet gotten to the level of evil desperation of Humphrey Bogart's character in *Treasure of the Sierra Madre*, I've already been driven to nightly larceny. Every evening I sneak up to the roof like a cat-burglar and filch a bucket of water from one of my neighbors' private tanks for my evening bucket bath. People who've never lived through a drought have no idea how much pure refreshment you can get from a washcloth.

I chose a different tank each day, lest my pilfering be noticed. If the rains begin tomorrow and continue until every reservoir in Taiwan overflows (which is exactly what happened last year in those halcyon days after a typhoon put downtown Taipei under several feet of water), there are some things I'll never take for granted again - little things, like being able to mop my floor, or to wash my hands after cleaning out the kitty litter box.

As Taiwan's reservoirs reach their own dead storage levels, people find different ways to deal with the looming probability of an ever-worsening crisis; temples from Tainan to Keelung are holding ceremonies to beseech the gods for rain, pouring water over cut-out representations of the island in hopes that the gods get the hint. Up in the mountains, aboriginals of various tribes are practicing their ceremonial rain dances. And me, well, after I finish this little essay, I'll be heading up to the roof to perform a little rain dance of my own. But I'm bringing up a bucket and a wrench, in case the dance fails. After all, the gods help those who help themselves. ❖

# Strange Foreign Person

Foreigners living in Taiwanese cities get stared at a lot; it's a fact of life in Asia. In Taipei, a city whose roads are choked with taxis, buses, and millions of $CO_2$ spurting scooters, anyone whose daily commute is done on skates is bound to get some funny looks. When the skater in question happens to have blue eyes and hair past his tattoo-covered shoulders, the Taiwanese consider this occurrence - barely registering a blink in the States - an actual newsworthy event.

In Taipei, my daily skate commute takes me down Wulai Road, a fairly steep mountain road, repaved since last year's typhoon, onto Bei Shing Avenue, a wide, traffic filled street that runs from the suburb of Hsintien into the heart of Taipei. Generally speaking, people give me a wide berth on the mountain road, shouting out encouragements like, "Very good!" and "Hello!" as they pass. I was pushing back up the hill one day last month when the community gatekeeper ran out of his hut to meet me. He seemed excited about something.

"Hello! Hello! A man from TV came here, wants me to give you his number! Here."

I called the number, which had been hastily scrawled on a

napkin, and was soon in touch with a reporter from Formosa Television.

"Do you remember me?" he asked. "I yelled 'hello' in English at you on Wulai Road today."

"Um...sure," I lied.

"I am in charge of producing features on interesting people for Formosa Television's Nightly News Hour. I was hoping I could do a feature on you for next week."

"Sounds good," I said. "What do I need to do?"

"We want to come to your apartment, interview you about skating, then follow you around as you go down the hill on Wulai Road and then through the city."

"Will you pay me?"

"No," he answered. "But you will be famous throughout Taiwan!"

I thought about it for a minute. After six years in this town, I was getting my 15 minutes of fame.

"OK," I said.

When the arranged day came, my new friend showed up at my house with camera crew in tow, and after a quick cup of tea and offering of cigarettes all around, we were off.

For the next three hours, I was filmed putting my skates on, getting into a crouch to maximize speed down Wulai Road,

*Strange Foreign Person*

towing onto the side of the press van, zooming through thickets of buses, taxis and motorcycles (from a variety of angles), and scaring the bejesus out of a hapless Taiwanese woman by coming to a screeching T-stop in front of her and asking her to marry me at once, "So I can stay in your country."

Okay, the last bit was my idea, but the film crew loved it, and so did all my friends who saw it that night on TV (except for my girlfriend, who hit me with a sneaker). Foreigners making spectacles of themselves are a popular form of entertainment in Taiwan, and the 90 second segment the film crew boiled down from our three hours of in-line shenanigans (aptly titled "*Gwei Lao-wai*" - strange foreign person) was a big hit. But the reason I wound up taking up a minute and a half of the collective consciousness of Formosa TV's viewers wasn't thanks solely to my face - I've been white for six years in this country without getting my mug on TV for it - it was because I was, according to the news crew, the first person they'd seen who was crazy enough to skate through Taipei's notoriously chaotic traffic.

"No Taiwanese would ever do this," one of the photographers told me.

But that's where he was wrong, and the people of Taiwan are in for a big surprise in the years to come. You see, in-line skating is big in Taiwan, and getting more so every year, but primarily among children. On any weekend day (and some weekday evenings), children by the hundreds, between the ages of six and thirteen, fill Chiang Kai-shek Memorial, Sun Yat-sen Hall, and other parks around Taipei. The kids come to take skating lessons, play hockey, or just tear-ass around in their mid-to-high priced skates, six-joint protective padding, and Hello Kitty helmets.

But kids grow fast, and as these kids grow, they'll find the parks that once seemed infinitely large have become boringly small. One day, armed with skating skills far superior to my own, they'll take to the streets - first to the alleyways, and then to the major avenues that make up this bustling Asian metropolis. Throngs of adolescent skaters will clog the intersections, motorcyclists will have to be on the lookout for unwanted hitchhikers towing rides, and one oddly-hued skater zooming down Wulai Road won't even be worth a second glance. ❖

# Fight Club

"In this corner, from New York, U.S.A., weighing 60 kilograms...Joshua!"

It was a hot August night in Taipei, and I was about to be beaten up in public, perhaps severely. Standing across the ring, if you could call a square taped on a cement barroom floor a ring, stood a teenaged kid with a mean, hungry glint in his eyes. He was pounding his gloves together in anticipation, and his message was all too clear - "White boy, you're going down." My last shred of confidence evaporated.

Dear Jesus, where had this madness begun? Was my strange, self destructive approach to journalism somehow involved? Did I really need to ask myself that?

I had heard about the club from some friends in Taipei who told me about a local bar that hosted an amateur boxing night every Saturday. From what I'd heard, participants were generally overworked Taiwanese businessmen letting off steam in a completely controlled environment, with regulation gloves and padded helmets. Why not write a story Hemingway-style, I thought, from the inside out. I'd made many a Taiwanese businessman burst into tears simply by refusing to let them pick up the dinner check. How hard could it be to beat one in a boxing ring?

Finding the place wasn't easy. I'd only had the vaguest idea of where to look - somewhere around the Technology Building Subway Station on Fushing Road. I set out around sundown with my friend, Kyle. Kyle had insisted on hitting me several times over the course of the day so I'd "be able to take a punch." It was only by sheer luck that we managed to spot the silver letters VS inlaid on the round handle of a silver door located in the far corner of the lobby of a non-descript Taiwanese office building. The place was locked up, but the doorman told us to come back after nine.

We got back around nine to find the chest-high VS sign up and the door leading into the basement open. It was still early, and the place was quiet. Kyle sat down and ordered a Coke while I scoped the place out. A decent sized basement club, the VS was separated into two rooms. Over to the left of the coat check counter (which doubles as a weigh in station on fight night) was a large chill-out space complete with low-slung chairs surrounding a dozen or so tables and some plush couches over by the walls. There was also a large-screen TV hanging from the ceiling. The main room had a dance floor, a DJ station with two turntables, long counters along one of the walls, and a stone bar that must have cost a fortune. Behind the bar was Jo, a stunningly gorgeous bartender who was glad to talk up the positive aspects of the club's most popular event.

"It really isn't violent at all. Most of the people who compete are just regular people, businessmen mostly, though sometimes women fight, too," she said. "Amateur boxing helps them to let off some steam."

*Fight Club*

Vincent Dai, the club's manager, told me that the club had been holding Fight Night every Saturday for about six months.

"The event has become increasingly popular with Westerners living in Taiwan," he said. "They think it is like that movie *Fight Club*, with bare knuckles and no rules, but that isn't at all the case. All our fights are two minutes, opponents are paired by weight class, and we use regulation ten-ounce gloves and padded helmets."

There was some prize money involved, he told me, a few thousand *kuai* for the most wins accumulated at the end of the month. But everything about the club was strictly amateur. "And most importantly, it stays friendly. No grudge matches."

Then he mentioned that, in addition to the professional referee, the club also employed two bouncers to make sure everything stayed friendly.

At around eleven, people began to arrive, and by midnight, the place was packed. I scanned the faces of the patrons, seeing among them not one who looked like he'd ever even owned a tie. These were no businessmen; these were hardened street punks. My mindless bravado faded like a cheap dye job.

If the sight of my potential opponents shook my poise, the next person I ran into shattered it. He was a stocky, well groomed American who bore the look of a man who had broken many a brick in his life. But his appearance wasn't what scared me. I could tell by the way he was dressed that he hadn't come to brawl. It was what he said that threw me into a blind panic.

"A mouthpiece isn't there to protect the teeth. It's to protect you from biting your tongue in half when you get hit in the jaw...I've seen it happen...very hard to stop the flow of blood from the tongue."

Bill was a lawyer and former kickboxing champion. He'd heard about the club, and wanted to see if the place was as colossally stupid as it sounded to a man with years of experience in competitive fighting.

"Even in a controlled situation, with experienced fighters, padded rings and professional referees, injuries are bound to happen," he said gravely. "Here, in a barroom situation with concrete floors, no mouthpieces, and untrained combatants...it's a disaster waiting to happen. You really should reconsider."

But it was too late for me to back down, so I accepted Bill's offer of a quick sidewalk sparring session, complete with ongoing safety commentary.

"Keep relaxed. Keep a good posture," he told me, showing me some rudimentary blocks and jabs. "And for god's sake, keep your mouth shut so you don't bite your tongue in half."

A half hour later, I was confident of being able to survive the match and not much else. We headed back downstairs to find that the dance floor had been cleared and a makeshift boxing ring had been marked with white tape on the floor. The air was charged as the referee pushed through the crowd and began the big wind up. He explained the rules, first in Taiwanese, then in Mandarin.

"No hitting below the belt. No elbows, knees or feet. No back of the head blows. Cross the white line once, a warning!

Twice, disqualification!"

He said one more thing, and I could swear his tone was more than a bit sarcastic.

"I see that we have some foreign friends signed up tonight. Very good! We love watching our foreign friends fight here at the VS club, don't we?"

At this the crowd cheered wildly, and I felt the hairs on the back of my neck stand up as the first combatants were called into the ring.

The first contest was between two young, scrawny teenagers who looked like they were barely out of high school. They didn't box so much as flail wildly. I began to feel encouraged, figuring that I could have handled either of them. As I was contemplating this, the referee spoke up again.

"Uh-oh, our next match-up is between a foreigner and a local - that's the best kind of fight!"

"Calling into the ring...Joshua!"

The crowd was screaming as I pressed my way into the taped-off ring. As one of the bouncers fitted me into a sweaty pair of gloves and sparring helmet, I sized up my opponent. He was taller than I was, and had a vicious look about him that made the previous two fighters look downright angelic. The bell rang. I gulped. He snarled, and ran straight at me, swinging.

Within seconds, I was on the defensive. I'd forgotten everything I'd been taught about offence, and was reduced to just blocking my face. The strobe lights were blinding and I could barely see the punches coming at me. I felt one land on top of my head, and when I swung out to retaliate, another hit me in the jaw, rattling my teeth. More rained down upon my head and the back of my neck, and I instinctively got into a clinch to avoid further punishment. The referee pulled us apart.

"Are you OK?" he asked.

I then remembered the last bit of advice Bill had given me; tap out if you're outclassed. My opponent was declared winner by surrender, and given as a prize a large bath towel with the Tiger Beer logo. I was given a washcloth with the same logo, and left to slink back into the crowd. It would be up to Kyle to regain some lost prestige for Taipei's foreign community, which he did, much to the chagrin of the assembled Taiwanese crowd.

While from ringside, his match looked like total chaos, Kyle told me that he'd developed a strategy while watching the other two fights.

"I went in with the idea that it would be a boxing match, but when I realized it would be more of a sumo match, I decided to just let my opponent tire himself out, scare him with a few hard punches, then push him out of the ring. It hurt like hell, but it was worth it."

*Fight Club*

All told, there were less than half a dozen matches that night, and there weren't any female competitors. After the last fight was over, a very dangerous floorshow began in which the bartenders juggled bottles of flaming alcohol. This seemed to me a bad idea of entertainment in a crowded basement stocked with alcohol, drunks, and no fire exits.

Saying goodnight to Kyle, I walked out of the Vacuum Space and into the sweltering embrace of a Taipei summer night, leaving with teeth, tongue, and self esteem more-or-less intact. I'd done what I'd come to do, and if I didn't get the story I intended to get, it was only because the actual facts had intervened. There'd been no thrill of victory, and no real agony in my defeat, but only a reminder of what I should have known all along. I was too pretty - and too old - to be a prize fighter. ✤

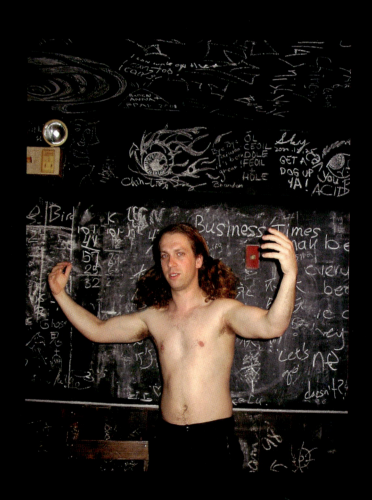

# Love Hotel Etiquette

The short stretch of light rail that stretches between the Peitou and Hsin Peitou Stations is an anomaly. Since it is not even long enough for the train to get up any speed and connects Peitou to a neighborhood that isn't populated enough to really warrant its own station, one tends to wonder just why this strange little appendage exists. Suspicious souls might suspect that the ugly specter of political pork barreling in the extreme reared its head mightily in its construction, but such cynicism should be quickly dispelled by the realization that this amazingly expensive stretch of rail exists for one purpose alone - to make it that much more convenient for you, personally, to get to Hsin Peitou - Hot Spring Love Hotel Capital of the World.

A few hours at one of these places will set you back between 400 and 800 NT (the "take a rest rate"), and an evening will cost you and a loved one between 1200 and 2300. A word of advice: go on a weeknight for the discounts, and spend the extra money; while the difference in price between the cheap and the chic may be an hour or two of pay, it'll be worth it just to see the look on your loved one's face upon seeing the 21-inch stereophonic TV and a natural hot-spring fed Jacuzzi big enough to float a small fishing boat. And nothing says class like his-and-her individually wrapped toothpicks.

The hot spring love hotels of Hsin Peitou are your home away from home, except you won't have to clean up, and, unlike your nosy neighbors, the desk clerk will not judge you as you leave in the morning after a night of loving debauchery with the him, her or combination thereof of your choice. The facilitation of your enjoyment is all that concerns them, and the strange, crooked smiles on their customers' faces are the only thanks they require. This leaves you free to shed your inhibitions to the fullest extent allowed by the law and/or your personal dogma.

Losing one's inhibitions is easier said than done (except when drunk, when the opposite is often true). As I walked out of one after a particularly decadent evening, I found myself wondering, "What will the cleaning lady think of the half eaten chunks of Laughing Cow Cheese scattered around the bed? Will the manager be informed about the quantity of cheap supermarket caviar floating in the Jacuzzi?" In my naiveté, I actually initiated conversation with the cleaning lady on the way to the elevator, to apologize for the extreme untidiness with which she was about to deal.

"Oh, *na-li, na-li!*" she laughed. "Our only concern is that you had a good time. Leave the mess to us, and come back again soon." A far cry indeed from the words spoken by my parents the morning after my last sleepover party.

Of course, there are other activities available in Hsin Peitou for those disinclined to debauchery. There are several public hot springs in and around the oddly named Anti-Calamity Park directly across from the station, and nestled as it is in the armpit of beautiful Yaming Mountain, Hsin Peitou is an excellent point from which to start any number of hikes. Several of the bigger hotels in the neighborhood also offer both public and private hot springs, separated by gender or for the exclusive use of the paying customer and guest. There is also a long-standing rumor that some of these seedier places will, for a fee, provide a bathing companion for the undiscriminating gentleman, but I'd advise against that. Love, like advice, is best appreciated when freely given. ❖

# Water Running Up

Motorists driving the highways and byways of America have a plethora of roadside oddities to entice them to slow down for a stretch and drop a few dollars on entrance fees and trinkets. Taiwan, however, isn't well known for its abundance of bizarre roadside tourist attractions. You won't find signs on the Sun Yat-sen Freeway advertising stuff like "Only 50 kilometers to the Fabulous Tofu Palace" or "World's Largest Betel Nut, Next Right."

Though deprived of strange roadside oddities, Taiwan isn't entirely devoid of them. I was naturally intrigued when on a motorcycle trip around Taitung on the east coast highway, I came upon a sign reading in both Chinese and English: "Water Running Up - 500 meters." The arrow was pointing west, so I turned off the main highway and rode for a half a kilometer until I came to a small, winding stream running down from - or up to - a hill. Next to this was a parking lot with a noodle stand and a stall selling coconuts. A couple dozen bemused tourists milled around while the more adventurous among them actually lay next to the little brook, using their bodies as carpenter's levels to physically ascertain the level of the land while dipping a hand into the water.

I walked over to the stream and sat down. The ground was indeed on a tilt. I stuck my hand in, determining that the water was cold and indeed flowing, in complete defiance of a most basic natural law, up. I followed the stream up the hill, dipping my hand in at regular intervals; each dip drew the same result - water running up. A quarter of a kilometer or so up the hill, the brook narrowed to a trickle and disappeared beneath some rocks. I walked back down the hill with the unsettling feeling that everything I knew might be wrong, and bought a fried oyster cake from a guy with a deep-fat fryer on wheels and a coconut from a woman sitting on the ground next to him.

"Lived around here all my life," the woman told me, handing me a coconut with a straw sticking out of it, "and this stream has always done that. Water runs up. Not down, up. It's a real mystery of nature."

I finished my oyster pancake and coconut, paid, and headed back to the highway, leaving the supernatural tourist trap behind and thinking now I've seen just about everything. ✤

# Green Island: Ready for the Big Time

It's a clear blue morning on Taiwan's southeastern shore. I'm standing at the foot of the dock in Fukang. A preternaturally pale middle-aged Taiwanese man wearing lipstick, eye liner and a stuffed push-up bra, hands me my ferry ticket. It's my second trip to Green Island, home of Taiwan's once-feared political prison, and once again a transvestite is involved.

I'd last come two years before, researching the Green Island diving scene for a travel magazine. I'd broken into the courtyard of the Oasis Hotel, the facetiously named political prison. Once a fearsome symbol of repression, it now stood in disrepair, closed to the public. I was prepared for ghosts, but certainly nothing living; I was thus naturally surprised to run smack into Taiwanese Vice President Annette Lu, herself a former inmate, with a small television crew in tow. She spotted me before I could skulk back into the shadows, so I decided to make the most of it.

"Madame Vice President," I said in my most obsequious Mandarin. "I'm a foreign journalist, and I'm here doing research for a book on Taiwan's history."

Madame Vice President just laughed.

"Then you must know that once I was put behind these very walls for advocating democracy."

Smelling an interview, I suggested that it must be bittersweet indeed to revisit the place where she'd suffered so greatly.

"Oh, I suffered, all right," she replied. "Room service was terrible, darling!"

My contemplation of the veep's glibness was interrupted by giggling from her entourage. But the man behind the camera was less amused. "Why is this *ahdogha* (foreigner) on the set?"

"You have to leave now, darling," the veep told me, winking. "I've got to go to work."

It was then that I noticed that Annette Lu's Adam's apple was bigger than mine. The tearful return of former political detainee to her place of captivity was a sham, part of a comedy sketch in progress. And the woman to whom I'd been directing my obsequiousness was neither woman nor politician, but a transvestite who made a tidy living impersonating famous Taiwanese women for laughs on late-night television. What a difference a few decades free of martial law can make in a once-uptight society.

Back to the present day, and my latest encounter with the gender-bent is behind me, along with mainland Taiwan. December is low season on Green Island, and disembarking from the ferry, I have my pick of scooters. I score a 125cc Sanyang for 200 NT (USD 6), and the old woman renting bikes doesn't ask to see my passport.

"Why bother?" she laughs. "You can't get the bike off the

island."

Nor is there much chance of hiding the bike on the island. Circumnavigating the island takes a mere 45 minutes on the one coastal road, which meanders like a drunken snake in pursuit of its own tail, offering some of the most astonishingly gorgeous coastal scenery in Taiwan - beautiful rocky coves, lush windswept hills and high stones named after mythical animals and fairy tale characters. The only other road on the island leads up Amei Mountain, a peak with a 360 degree view of the ocean. Low season also means I have my pick of hotels. I settle on the Tu Yie Shan Zhuan, a yellow-tiled, newly built five-story hotel overlooking scenic Kungkuan Cape, a steal at 1000 NT per night. After dinner at a local restaurant (wild deer hotpot, a local specialty), I head out to visit the famed sea-water hot-springs on the island's southern tip.

One of only three sea-water springs in the world, the Chaorih (Sunrise) Springs is a mixture of old and new spa design. On the dark end of the beach sit three ancient circular stone pits filled with geothermal seawater. Closer to the road is a modern complex containing a series of interconnected modern tile pools ranging in temperature from just above freezing to just below scalding. Also in the complex are a number of artfully shaped artificial privacy grottos, and three massage showers, their overhead pipes jetting down hot spring water at jackhammer frequencies.

I run into a half-dozen expat English teachers at the spa, down for some weekend snorkeling with their Taiwanese girlfriends. I try to chat them up about coral conditions, but it's too late; alcohol and hot water have made them indolent, and the closest thing to information I get is, "Lovely coral...mate... good as th' Philippines." After two hours spent alternating between being relaxed and pummeled by water, I'm feeling lethargic too. While I slowly ride through the moonlight, the only other living being I pass is a small wild deer, possibly an orphan in search of missing relatives.

While most tourists are lured by scenery, sea and spa, the name Green Island will always bear association with Taiwan's political history. This is because its most famous landmark is the political prison which once housed those considered enemies by the Kuomintang during Taiwan's White Terror period - Chiang Kai-shek's final play for power in a war he'd already lost. Some, like writer Bo Yang (author of *The Ugly Chinaman*) and Vice President Annette Lu (the real Lu, not her transvestite doppelganger), had lived to tell their tales. Others weren't so fortunate. The museum takes up one wing of the prison, a subtle, understated monument with pictures of those imprisoned and killed lining the walls. More somber than the museum is the prison itself, which sits much as it did decades ago, save for two differences - except for the occasional visitor, the prison is empty, and the cell doors and gates separating the wings stand eternally flung open.

Though the weather is fine, and most of the shops offering scuba and snorkeling excursions are still operating, I decide to stay on land for the rest of the day. It's just as well; had I gone diving, I may have wound up crashing a wedding party, for a quarter mile out and 90 feet below the waves, a most unusual ceremony is taking place as Kevin and Claire Yang are being locked in matrimonial bliss in an undersea wedding. I run into the couple a few hours later as wedding dress, tuxedo and cummerbund are hanging out to dry. They are both professional divers, and the ceremony (witnessed by 66 divers and solemnized by a minister from Hong Kong) is the second such ceremony to be held off the shores of Green Island.

*Green Island: Ready for the Big Time*

"This really is a fabulous spot for scuba diving, and we've dived all over the world," says Kevin. "Our vows to each other were written on waterproof cards and we used sign language to say 'I do.'"

"I feel like the sea-goddess Matsu blesses our union," adds Claire.

The comment surprises me, as the vicar's presence suggests that the couple is Christian.

"Oh, we're Buddhists," Claire clarifies. "But we couldn't find a scuba-diving monk."

I spend the rest of the day hiking in verdant green hills, climbing up crumbling guard towers and into abandoned artillery trenches, all relics of the island's years as a prison and military outpost. Green Island will probably never make Asian tourism's A-list; sadly, this is Taiwan's lot. But as long as there are travelers who appreciate lush hills and amazing hot-springs, blue skies and coral-filled seas, history and transvestites, Taiwan's version of Robben Island will never want for guests. ❖

# Nighthawks at the Night Market

Midnight in Taipei, and winter was approaching faster than anticipated. An arctic cold front had just blown in from the mainland, letting me know that I'd put off buying a winter quilt a few days too long. My cell phone was broken from having dropped it down a flight of stairs, and I had a powerful craving for some squid on a stick.

So it was off to the night market, where night and day are reversed, commerce is king, and at midnight the lights from a hundred shops and stalls are bright enough to block out the moon.

The cab lets me off at the market's edge, and dozens of smells immediately begin competing for my attention - sausages broiling on an open flame, yams cooking in a gigantic stone kiln mounted on the back of a three wheeled scooter, exhaust fumes from scooters being revved aggressively by teenagers at crosswalks, and stinky tofu. I don't spot a squid vendor, so I buy a stick of marinated chicken buttocks. It has a strange texture, fleshy yet crunchy with softened cartilage.

Hunger sated, I work my way through the market, looking into the stalls on the sides for a quilt vendor and a cell-phone fixer, trying to ignore the hawking of the freelance vendors selling stuff I don't need.

"Hey, foreigner! Buy some socks! Four pair, 100 NT."

I guess I do need socks. The ones I have are wearing mighty thin in the heel.

"Five pairs, 100 NT!" I shout at the vendor, a middle aged woman standing on a ladder.

"No way. Ten pair, 200 NT."

I start to walk away.

"OK! Come back! Five pair, 110 NT!"

A good deal; I really do need new socks.

Though I was cold at home, the night market produces a climate of its own. Up ahead one stall is selling alarm clocks, all ringing simultaneously as if to advertise their effectiveness.

"*O-HIO!*" (good morning) screams one shaped like a Japanese cartoon character famed for prowess in flatulence. "Time to wake up, time to wake up, time to get out of bed," sings a plastic dog in a 45 RPM falsetto. A few plastic roosters screech "cock-a-doodle-doo," cows moo, bells ring and birds twitter. Though it would seem a cacophony anywhere else, at the night market the endless chiming fits nicely with the overall din.

I find a stall advertising cell phone repairs. The proprietor, a teenager with earrings and dyed blonde hair, seems uncomfortable at first, as if seeing a white face reminds him of the

*Nighthawks at the Night Market*

hundreds of hours he's wasted in forced and futile English study. He tries to sell me a new phone for 4000 NT, but settles on fixing the old one for 400.

"Leave the phone with me and come back in half an hour," he tells me, and I'm out again in the sea of people searching for something to keep me warm at home on this cold, cold night.

"Puppies! Puppies! Adorable Puppies."

Not that, however. I barely look at the thuggish looking teenager hawking puppies in the middle of the lane, and he barely looks back at me, knowing I don't fit the profile of a likely late night spur of the moment puppy customer.

A booming sound from three stalls up sends me ducking for cover, and seconds later, the smell of *bong lipang* - "exploding fragrant rice" wafts through the market. It says a lot about a country when people in a crowded market don't mind snacks in which loud explosions are part of the preparation. The Buddhist nun chanting with her alms bowl ten feet away doesn't even seem to notice. I buy a warm brick of the stuff for later before finding a stall selling winter quilts. While mobile phones are typically a young man's racket, quilts are traditionally an older person's game. With a minimum of haggling, I wind up with a thick quilt without any noisy cartoon characters before heading back to the phone guy, who hands me a now-working cell phone and takes most of the rest of my cash.

Mission accomplished, I push my way through the crowd back to the market's edge and hail a cab back home. In the taxi it occurs to me that I never did get my squid, but the thought soon passes. There'll be other nights for squid. ❖

# On the Mooch in Dihua Jie

In the week before Lunar New Year, I decided to go to the Dihua Market to research a lively yet informative article about shopping for gifts for upcoming festivities. This proved to be a difficult task, as I not only had almost no money in the bank, but had actually left my wallet at home, and had all of 95 NT making a lonely jangle against the keys in my jacket pocket. So shopping was out of the question. Dinner, however, would be literally thrust upon me, as the Dihua Market turns into a veritable moocher's paradise during the run up to Lunar New Year. Whether this was due to some long standing Taiwanese tradition or simple business acumen I can't say, but what I do know is that no visitor to the Dihua Market is permitted to leave hungry. As I walked through the packed streets of the market, all types of Chinese New Year treats were pressed my way for the sampling - milk chocolate from Japan, slices of salted Ilan duck meat on toothpicks, Dixie cups filled with diced abalone and shark's fin soup, and even bits of broiled pig's feet. And that was just for starters.

Although I was nigh penniless, the Dihua Market was a buffet trough through which I happily wallowed from beginning to end, allowing me to report with authority that pressed fish roe is a traditional gift that, while pricey, is cheaper than you'd expect a lung-sized chunk of caviar to be. A merchant of fine green teas assured me that a vacuum packed bag of green tea never fails to make a good impression with friends and relatives over the holiday season. Squid bits on a stick, broiled eel wrapped in seaweed, smoked oysters stuck on toothpicks - all these and more were thrust my way as I pushed through the festivities.

By the time I reached the end of the market, I was stuffed with strange samples and wired from endless mini Dixie cups of fine tea: oolongs, greens, mountains and even a few that tasted like mentholated grass. Sated, I thought I'd be able to just turn around and find my way back to the entrance. But the collective conscious of the market had other plans.

Under normal circumstances, Taiwanese people are adamant about not letting guests walk away hungrier than they were when they came. When the guest in question happens to be a foreigner, the tradition is especially strong, as if to say "the poor Westerner…he didn't seem to understand a thing we said, but at least he won't go telling people we let him starve." At the Dihua Market, this took on a whole new meaning as merchants refused to let someone walk away without sampling something.

"Try some broiled fish! It's from Japan. Very special."

"But I have no money," I protested.

"Eat now, come back and buy later!"

"Abalone! Dried scallops! Oolong teas - best quality!"

"But I'm a shameless grifter."

"Then eat more!"

Eventually the market let me through, stuffed with dried fish, octopus balls, chunks of abalone, seaweed, candies and even some very delicious (if not traditionally Taiwanese) cheesecake. In Beijing, Shanghai, or even San Francisco, the constant mingling of rich, poor and tourists makes beggars a fact of life. On Dihua Street, in the week before Lunar New Year, the problem is reversed. Saying no to an eight year old with a dirty, cherubic face and an outstretched palm is hard enough. Saying no to a gorgeous Taiwanese girl offering me a handful of dried squid proved nigh impossible, even after six mouthfuls of the stuff. I came hungry, and left stuffed, still carrying the same 95 NT with which I'd arrived. And contrary to the hackneyed cliché about Chinese food, I was still full an hour later. ❖

# Last Dance for the KMT

Taiwan's watershed legislative election is history, and the former martial-law era masters, the Kuomintang (KMT), who last year lost the presidency, has now lost control of the legislature as well. Where I live, the Sanchung District of Taipei County - a lower middle class neighborhood with strong Democratic Progressive Party (DPP) leanings - the KMT's loss has been greeted with fireworks, horn honking, and much celebratory drinking. I can only assume that Cable 8, the Taiwanese TV channel whose election night return reports have been read while a loop of "We Will Rock You" blares in the background, shares my neighbors' political leanings. While probably not Queen's intentions, the song's lyrics can be interpreted as a mantra against the KMT's fifty-year rule of dirty politics and mindless jingoism:

> *You got mud on your face*
> *You big disgrace*
> *Shaking your banner all over the place.*

Taiwanese elections are a noisy affair from beginning to end. Loudspeaker mounted campaign trucks filled with supporters have been prowling the streets nonstop for months, drowning out everything in their wake. Yesterday, I was in my fifth floor apartment on a long distance call to Singapore when one of these campaign screechers prowled by.

"What the hell was that?" my friend asked as soon as the noise had died down.

"Democracy," I answered.

Local pundits promised that this election would 'redraw the political landscape,' and they may be right. President Chen Shui-bian's term in office has so far been marked by near-impotence, as all his attempts at passing political and economic reform were blocked at every turn by an openly hostile KMT controlled legislature. While this election makes Chen's party the top dog in the Legislative Yuan, the DPP still lacks an outright majority, as many of the KMT's lost seats have gone to newly formed smaller parties. With whom these smaller parties will choose to ally themselves is the hot topic now, but everybody agrees that some serious horse trading is in Taiwan's political future.

It remains to be seen how mainland China's government will react to this sudden strengthening of President Chen's hand. To say that the Chinese Communist Party (CCP) holds Chen Shui-bian in contempt is an understatement. They like Chen less than they did his predecessor, Lee Tung-hui, who they regularly referred to with such charming sobriquets as "Japanese collaborator" and "Western / splittist puppet." While the mainland government has attempted to influence previous Taiwanese elections through action (offshore missile tests in 1996) and bluster (thinly veiled threats in 2000), this election marked a new, subtler strategy on their part.

As recently as two weeks ago, reports were leaked to the press of backroom CCP/KMT meetings, with the former offering "political and other kinds" of support to ensure the DPP's defeat at the polls. While this might seem strange to some Asia watchers - the CCP and the KMT spent a good chunk of the twentieth century trying to exterminate each other, nearly succeeding more than once - they do both profess to want to unite China and Taiwan under one flag (though they have differing ideas about the color of said flag). Still, while the CCP's plans may have been based on the time-honored strategy of befriending your enemy's enemy, this attempt, like others by mainland China to exert influence on a Taiwanese election, seems to have backfired.

When the votes were finally tallied, The KMT had lost its majority status to the DPP, with neither party holding an absolute majority thanks to strong showings by two newly created Taiwanese political parties - former KMT stalwart James Soong's People First Party, and former President Lee Tung-hui's newly formed Taiwan Solidarity Union - the genesis and allegiances of which can best be described as "complicated."

While the KMT's loss of power is certainly good news for Chen Shui-bian and the DPP, the new configuration of Taiwan's legislature presents uncertainties. While most Taiwanese hope for greater inter-party cooperation, some fear that the rise of smaller parties will lead to further government gridlock, the sort of which has been crippling Japan for over a decade. But here in my pro-DPP neighborhood, this is a worry for another day. Right now, their party has come out on top, and in Sanchung, it's all over but the shouting. Once that ends, maybe I'll be able to get some sleep. ❖

# Taiwan Speaks Up, Damn the Torpedoes

It was March 26th, 2005, and the streets of Taipei were choked with people from all over the island, citizens of a nation still known legally as the Republic of China (ROC) who had gathered in force to protest a new anti-secession law that had just been passed by the much larger People's Republic of China (PRC) less than 100 miles to the west. The wording of the law was purposely obtuse, but the overall gist was crystal clear - any declaration of independence by the government of the ROC would lead to a swift retaliation by the growing military of the PRC.

Were there a million people, as ROC President Chen Shui-bian had hoped for? Or was the number less by maybe half? Only people in helicopters or tourists gawking from the observation deck of the Taipei 101 Observatory or the now low-rent Shingong Tower can really guess. But there certainly were a lot of people, both dyed in the wool independence supporters and ordinary Taiwanese who just don't much like the menacing signals sent out by the Chinese Communist Party's anti-secession law (referred to by some in these parts as the Anschluss edict.)

The march began in a strange wagon wheel formation, with ten massive lines of people wearing green hats, blowing air horns and waving banners, starting at different points in the city and marching towards the Presidential Palace. Once there, Chen Shui-bian - both ROC President and precariously perched high priest of "all that is good and pro-Taiwan, while stopping just short of actually declaring independence" - would either speak or not. There was some confusion over this, but all were certain that he would sing. A-bian enjoys singing, and the buzz in the papers was that he'd written a song especially for the occasion based loosely on Bob Dylan's "Blowing in the Wind."

Each of the ten different starting points for the march represented one of the clauses in China's anti-secession law; on each spoke, the numbers could have easily been in the high tens of thousands or more, making the total number on this island of 20-some million impressive regardless of whether it actually reached one million. Many marchers waved flags with images of the leaf-shaped island. Other groups wielded banners reading "Taiwan is not China" and "Germany 1935 = China 2005." Some considered even this too subtle, choosing to voice themselves with the less eloquent but decidedly more direct message - "Fuck China."

But was this march really about declaring independence, an ominous move for all parties involved, maybe even the entire world economy? There were less than subtle clues to be found in the languages chosen by the sign-waving mob. Though the majority of signs were written in Chinese, every third or fourth sign was in English, with a few in French, or some other language directed towards the European Union. Indeed, much of the rhetoric of the rally seemed to be an equal part about making Taiwan's collective voice heard as sending any

*Taiwan Speaks Up, Damn the Torpedoes*

real message to China. Barred from most international decision-making bodies and abandoned diplomatically by all but a handful of countries, the Taiwanese have a powerful desire to be recognized, and certainly the new anti-secession law gives the island ample cause to expect support from any nation paying lip-service to the notion of democracy.

And what about this new law? Is it a step further in the direction of war, or is it, as one long term Taiwan-based expat expressed, quite the opposite: a canny ploy by moderates in Beijing to appease the Chinese militarists by setting down as an absolute red line any declaration of independence, thus allowing the status quo to continue while helping to isolate the hard-line pro-independence advocates in Taiwan? And if Chen knows this, might the whole march just be a convenient steam release to appease his own base? In other words, despite the current tension, might cooler heads prevail?

The afternoon before the march I'd been talking about just this topic with a fairly high ranking member of the DPP's inner circle, a young political operative who asked not to be identified by name. I'd been introduced to "Mr. Wu" through a friend as an American journalist. This fact alone would have made most in the pro-independence camp, who (naively or not) see America as a stalwart defender of democracy, feel quite comfortable about launching into the usual pro-independence spiel - Communist China is the great oppressor; Democratic Taiwan is the victim. So I was quite surprised when Mr. Wu started our conversation by telling me about a trip he'd just taken to Shanghai, comparing his last trip to others he'd taken during his university years and talking about how rapidly Chinese society was changing. When the discussion finally turned to politics, Mr. Wu was the picture of moderation. While neither confirming nor denying the protest-as-

steam-valve theory, he said he felt that both the passing of the law by Beijing and the timing of the march in Taipei were largely political, meant more for domestic and international consumption than to indicate any real change in policy. He'd traveled around China, and had had a good time, and felt that the resolution of the situation across the strait, whatever that resolution might be, could and should wait another generation, with neither side making any potentially foolish moves.

Quite a different tone was present on the streets the next day as DPP trucks whipped the crowd into anti-mainland chanting. When the spokes converged, President Chen, who'd marched on one of the main spokes surrounded by police, appeared larger than life on a huge monitor erected for the occasion. As promised, he made no speech, but did join chants of "What do we want from China? Peace!" before leading the assembled throng in a song about the praises of Taiwanese identity.

As the rally wound down, the masses dispersed in all directions, high on the buzz that good democracy ought to give those who take the time to participate. Snapping pictures in the post-rally glow, I - a conspicuous foreigner in a sea of green-clad Taiwanese faces - was thanked loudly and boisterously by no fewer than thirty people.

"Thank you for coming to Taiwan! Tell the people in your country who we are!"

Heading back to my hotel, it occurred to me that this may well have been the rally's main purpose - a public shout from the collective voice of Taiwan, a mass gathering to affirm to China, the world, and most importantly, themselves, that they refuse to be bullied in silence. Damn the torpedoes. ❖

**Final Words**

# Isle Formosa-An Inaccurate Historical Account

The island of Formosa, or Taiwan, is by geographical standards a veritable newborn. While geologists theorize that Taiwan was created by a massive underwater volcanic eruption a mere few million years ago, local legends maintain that Taiwan simply materialized one day in the mid 1400s beneath the outriggers of some bewildered Polynesian islanders out on a fishing expedition, who thereafter vowed never to set foot in the ocean again (a tradition that is still observed in Taiwan, especially during August, or 'ghost month').

Many years later, the first wave of settlers came from the Chinese mainland. These immigrants, called the Hakkas because of their annoying habit of clearing their throats before speaking, soon settled in the western lowlands, forcing the more polite natives into the eastern mountains to escape the noise.

Shortly after, settlers from Fukien province mistakenly landed on Taiwan due to a poorly drawn map sold to them by an unscrupulous American businessman offering them cheap

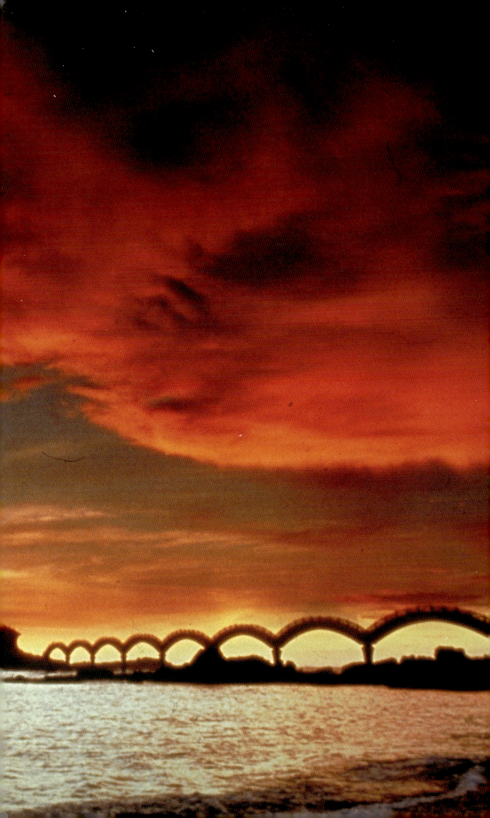

beachfront property in Hawaii. Refusing to admit their mistake, the Fukienese rounded up Hakka people by the dozen and forced them to perform crude hula dances and throw flowered leis everywhere. This incident has been a source of tension between the two groups ever since, and mentioning the name 'Don Ho' is often enough to provoke a severe beating in some neighborhoods.

Taiwan saw many major upheavals in the late nineteenth century, when the island was ceded to Norway after an all night gambling session between the last Dowager Empress of the Ming dynasty and a Norwegian conman called Hans. As part of this tragic bargain, all Taiwanese were forced to adopt Norwegian as their native language, drink heavily, eat lutefisk, and become suicidal during the long, dark winter months. This regime of terror lasted until 1945, when the cowed inhabitants discovered that Norway had not been a major world power since the mid tenth century, and had no means whatsoever of enforcing its edicts.

In 1949, a radio broadcast of HG Wells' immortal classic *The War of the Worlds* caused widespread panic in China, prompting millions to flee the mainland for Taiwan in hopes of surviving the impending Martian invasion. The population of Taiwan swelled to unprecedented numbers as a result, and architects throughout the island were forced to abandon long-held superstitions against the number four and design buildings with more than three floors.

Since then, the economy of Taiwan has swelled by over 1 billion percent, and even the most humble Taiwanese holds both a degree in electrical engineering and controlling interest in a mainland-based semiconductor factory. Taiwan boasts both breathtaking scenery and cosmopolitan cities, and plans are underway to build a road linking the two in the near future. ❖

Photos by Joshua Samuel Brown & ThingsAsian
Book design by Janet McKelpin
Editing assistance provided by Robert Tompkins
Printed in Hong Kong

Joshua Samuel Brown is a freelance writer who writes from various locations around Asia. He has written stories from the jungles of Laos and hobnobbed with high ranking communists in the underground buffet bunker of People's Daily in Beijing. His work has been seen in The South China Morning Post, The Hong Kong Daily Standard, The American Spectator, Beijing Scene, The Taipei Times, Boulder Weekly and The China Post. He is a semi regular contributor to various magazines in America and Asia.

Read short stories, articles, interviews and reviews by Joshua Samuel Brown at www.thingsasian.com

"Michael Palin Remembers Me"
"Searching for Pablo"
"Paradise Interrupted"
"The Feng Shui Detective Goes South"
"Gods and Monsters on the Mekong"
and more…

ThingsAsian Press

"*To know the road ahead, ask those coming back.*"
...Chinese proverb

East meets West at ThingsAsian Press, where the secrets of Asia are revealed by the travelers who know them best. Writers who have lived and worked in Asia. Writers with stories to tell about basking on the beaches of Thailand, teaching English conversation in the exclusive salons of Tokyo, trekking in Bhutan, haggling with antique vendors in the back alleys of Shanghai, eating spicy noodles on the streets of Jakarta, photographing the children of Nepal, cycling the length of Vietnam's Highway One, traveling through Laos on the mighty Mekong, and falling in love on the island of Kyushu.

Inspired by the many expert, adventurous and independent contributors who helped us build ThingsAsian.com, our publications are intended for both active travelers and those who journey vicariously, on the wings of words.

ThingsAsian Press specializes in travel stories, photo journals, cultural anthologies, destination guides and children's books. We are dedicated to assisting readers explore the cultures of Asia through the eyes of experienced travelers.